The Coming
CASHLESS
SOCIETY

Thomas Ice & Timothy Demy

HARVEST HOUSE PUBLISHERS
Eugene, Oregon 97402

Cover by Terry Dugan Design, Minneapolis, Minnesota

THE COMING CASHLESS SOCIETY

Copyright © 1996 by Harvest House Publishers
Eugene, Oregon 97402

Library of Congress Cataloging-in-Publication Data

Ice, Thomas.
    The coming cashless society / Thomas Ice & Timothy Demy.
        p.   cm.
    Includes bibliographical references.
    ISBN 1-56507-523-4 (alk. paper)
      1. Electronic funds transfers—Social aspects.   I. Demy, Timothy
J.   II. Title.
HG1710.I28   1996
303.48'33—dc20   96-18226
                                        CIP

Printed in the United States of America.

96 97 98 99 00 01 02 / BF / 10 9 8 7 6 5 4 3 2 1

To Dr. Tim LaHaye,
a man of uncommon vision for ministry
and one who has steadfastly loved and proclaimed
the hope of our Lord's soon coming.

Acknowledgments

This work was originally the idea of Bill Jensen at Harvest House Publishers. The authors are grateful to him and the rest of the staff for their confidence in our ability to produce this volume under rigorous deadlines. There are always many people behind the scenes who help in numerous ways in bringing a book to completion. Betty Fletcher, Carolyn McCready, and LaRae Weikert have been especially accommodating at Harvest House as they juggled several of our projects within their already-overburdened work load. We would especially like to thank Gary Stewart and Jim Ellis for their prayers and encouragement throughout the process. In addition to praying for the project, Tim's parents, Millard and Pauline Demy, tracked down several of the books and articles for us, freeing us from numerous hours of footwork so that we could press ahead with the writing.

Thanks finally to our wives, Janice Ice and Lyn Demy, perhaps the strongest and best critics of all.

"Cash has been the root of much social and economic evil. Some have advocated simply abolishing it, thus leaving the populace to use other existing non-cash payment media. The emergence of electronic funds-transfer technology, however, makes it possible to change the nature of money and divorce it from evil."

— David R. Warwick
The Cash-Free Society

"For the love of money is a root of all sorts of evil, and some by longing for it have wandered away from the faith, and pierced themselves with many a pang."

— The Apostle Paul
1 Timothy 6:10

Contents

Introduction

As you read these words, you have either recently purchased this volume or are considering its purchase. How did you or how will you pay for it? Cash, check, credit card? How did or how will the salesperson complete the transaction? Electronic cash register, hand-held UPC scanner? What about the inventory system required to reorder the book? How complex do you think it has become? This book is about these kinds of questions. It is about what is commonly known as the "cashless society" and some of its ramifications.

What would happen if you were told that you would no longer be able to use currency, coins, or other types of paper for all of your economic transactions? Instead, you would be required to use electronic technology for every transaction you made, large or small. Would you welcome such a move or feel uneasy about it? How would it relate to your views of privacy, freedom, and security? These are some of the issues we will address in the following pages.

This book is a contemporary evaluation of the state of technology, especially as it relates to the business transactions of everyday life, as seen through the grid of biblical prophecy. We believe that the Bible speaks not only to the present, but also to the future. How we live our lives today and how we prepare for tomorrow is very telling. The choices we make each day have not only temporal consequences but, in many instances, eternal consequences as well.

The apostle Paul wrote to Timothy about economic choices, stating:

But those who want to get rich fall into temptation and a snare and many foolish and harmful desires which plunge men into ruin and destruction. For the love of money is a root of all sorts of evil, and some by longing for it have wandered away from the faith, and pierced themselves with many a pang. But flee from these things, you man of God; and pursue righteousness, godliness, faith, love, perseverance and gentleness (1 Timothy 6:9-11).

As you read these pages and evaluate your own present and future, may Paul's words remain ever present in your mind, for someday those who reject his words will follow the words of another leader—one who will lead them to an eternal destiny apart from God.

1

The Dawn of a New Era or the Eve of Destruction?

THE EXPLOSION OF TECHNOLOGY

Hurry up, Andrea. We've got to leave, or we're going to be late! We have to stop by the ATM to get money for the conference fees, and we need gas too." Paul was staring at his watch when Andrea finally appeared at the front door. "If you wouldn't spend so much time surfing the Net, you'd have been ready earlier. It's not like I didn't have a full day myself," he muttered.

With one of the biggest names in prophecy coming to their community for a seminar on the pros and cons of the coming "cashless society," Paul and Andrea wanted to be on time and get as close to the front of the auditorium as possible. They were both looking forward to this as much as they had for the prophecy conferences they attended while in college. Neither of them wanted to miss a moment!

After acquiring crisp new bills from the ATM, they stopped to buy gas, sliding their new debit card through the slot at the pump before heading to the church. They arrived just a couple of minutes before the program began. When Paul reached the registration table, he politely offered two fresh $20 bills to one of the coordinators to cover the cost for Andrea and himself. The woman refused the cash.

"Sir, since this is a conference on the cashless society, we decided to have the participants experience as much of the future as possible. What I need from you is a credit card or debit card. I can't take cash or checks, and I'm not prepared to make any change. By the way, here are your national identification cards. Without them, neither you nor Andrea will be able to purchase refreshments or conference materials. During the seminar, the speaker will tell you more about the personal information that is encoded on the card, which we obtained from your preregistration forms and some other sources."

Amazed and a little bewildered, Paul and Andrea paid their fees, picked up their notebooks, and entered the auditorium. What they saw as they worked their way through the crowd was unusual for an event at church. The usual seating design had been altered. Rather than rows of chairs lined up from front to rear, long tables were set up throughout the auditorium with microphones on them. As they looked toward the front, they saw the podium had been replaced with a large screen.

"Maybe he's going to show a video or slides," Andrea remarked. "Move up closer."

Their pastor soon came out and requested that everyone take a seat. "We told you this was going to be an unusual seminar on prophecy and that we would give you a realistic view of what the world might soon be like in these last days before the rapture and in the period following it. You experienced one aspect of this cashless society in the foyer as you registered. If you want to purchase any materials at the break or the conclusion of the seminar, you'll be reminded again of what the future holds.

"In front of you is a microphone and microcamera that will allow visual and oral interaction with our speaker tonight during the question-and-answer segment. Simply key the mike and begin to speak; our lecturer will see you, hear your question, and respond from his office on Long Island. Please keep your questions brief and to the point. There are six other sites around the country joining us tonight, and we don't want one person or one site dominating the interaction. Also joining us by satellite are participants from the new biblical study center in Jerusalem. It's very late for you folks there, but we're glad to have you with us.

"Now let me introduce you to our speaker for the evening. ..."

Andrea and Paul were dumbfounded. They had just been introduced to a cashless society with telecommunication and video conferencing technology that made it unnecessary for the speaker to leave the comfort of his office. They had been required to carry a personal history with them on an identification card, without which they were unable to conduct routine commercial interactions or obtain food and beverages. On the way home, the couple stopped by a local pastry shop for coffee and pie and to talk about the evening. When the waitress brought the check, they still had all their unused cash, and even change for a tip!

"It was a strange feeling. Some of it was okay, but some of it was overwhelming," mused Andrea.

"I know what you mean," Paul chimed in. "Maybe the future is already here."

Nightmare or Nirvana?

Paul is right. The future *is* now. What was once only science fiction has become reality. And we are left with important questions about the implications, promise, and dangers of these technological breakthroughs.

The phenomenal growth of the computer and software markets has brought unbelievable wealth and status to many. Consider Microsoft founder, Bill Gates. He believes that technology can be used to usher in a better world. For the past 2½ decades, Gates has been on what he describes as "an incredible adventure."

Because of what he has seen, what he has accomplished, and what he believes about technology and the future, he confidently states, "I think this is a wonderful time to be alive. There have never been so many opportunities to do things that were impossible before."[1]

On the other hand, the explosion of technology in the last few years was apparently so repulsive to one individual that he undertook a one-man war against its spread. In his rambling manifesto published in the press and on the Internet, the Unabomber wrote that "the Industrial Revolution and its consequences have been a disaster for the human race. . . . The continued development of technology will worsen the situation. . . . We therefore advocate a revolution against the industrial system. . . . Its object will be to overthrow not governments but the economic and technological basis of the present society."[2]

Technology: Hero or Nero?

When was the last time you used a slide rule or even saw one? It has probably been quite a while unless you've recently cleaned out your high school memorabilia or visited a museum. The technology we use daily is changing so rapidly we can hardly keep up with it. Anyone who loves listening to music has probably spent a small fortune over the years on it. Unfortunately, if you are like us, the money has not been spent on expanding your musical library, but rather, on keeping current the ability to play your favorite songs. By the time you have bought the 45 singles, the $33\frac{1}{3}$ albums, the reel-to-reel tapes, the 4-track and 8-track tapes, the cassettes, and the CDs, you have spent a great deal of money just to stay up to date. And that's just technology for musical entertainment. Consider your computer and its upgrades: One day you are current and the next you are virtually obsolete. Who would have thought a gigabyte could be so important?

Will this new technology really make our lives better? If you have ever lost your money in a newspaper stand or had to clear the paper jam in a photocopy machine, you know the frustration of technology. But there is good too. Our "911" technology saves lives, as do astonishing breakthroughs in modern medicine.

In our everyday lives, it is inevitable that we will experience the limitations of our new inventions. Computers are great, until your hard drive crashes. We love our Macs and PCs until we ship them off for repairs and have to go looking for a typewriter or a pen that's not out of ink. Air conditioning is great until it breaks down in August and the repair service is out on a company picnic. Automobiles are wonderful until you are sitting on the side of the road in rush hour and the battery in your cellular phone is dead and the peppermint ice cream in the grocery bag is melting. Electronic transfers are quick and easy, until the money is deposited in another person's account and your check bounces.

Countless new developments in the realms of finance, economics, and technology are making the digital economy a reality. Electronic banking, debit cards, "smart" cards, and electronic money are becoming commonplace. Your local newspaper may bring the world to your doorstep, but the Internet brings it into your living room and den, allowing you not only to read about it, but also to interact instantaneously with it. A generation ago, many people feared the intrusion of "Big Brother" into their lives. Now the fear for many is that "Big Brother" may have a host of other intrusive siblings. Some observers of contemporary technological change believe that these are very unique times, so much so that in the realm of commerce, the inter-networked business "is as different from the corporation of the twentieth century as the latter was from the feudal craft shop."[3]

What should our attitude be toward these burgeoning changes? As we will see in the following pages, we cannot simply reduce it to a question of good or evil. Technology in itself, we believe, is neutral. However, we must recognize that because technology is created by flawed human beings, its use is affected by the moral condition of the human heart, and therefore subject to evil use. How then should Christians respond to technological advances in general and economic technology in specific?

Evil, we must emphasize, is a *theological* issue, not a *technological* one! Those who lack a proper theological framework erroneously assign evil (or virtue) to inanimate objects or tools, rather than to the human heart. Like any other tools of daily existence, technology is merely one means through which human desire is displayed.

A discussion of the coming cashless society must therefore include not only a present perspective of the technology itself, but also a prophetic perspective of its use. When we talk about technology and the present, we must address it in relation to human ethics and morality, but when we talk about technology and the future, we should relate it to biblical prophecy.

The Stage is Set

An understanding of the coming cashless society is necessary to gain proper perspective of our place in history. In order to gain such a perspective, we need God's viewpoint on earthly events, which we can draw from God's Word—the Bible.

It is clear that a cashless system will play a key role in the future, as prophesied in Scripture. It is also clear that current world developments indicate that we are rapidly approaching that time described in the Bible as the last days. Although there are some very good things about a cashless society, there are also some significant concerns, especially when looked at from a biblical perspective. Many students of prophecy see a cashless society as a sign of the approach of the end times and the coming of a world leader known as the Antichrist. Should this then have an effect on the way we live and the economic choices we make?

Today, the world is similar to a stage being set for a great drama. The major actors are standing in the wings waiting for their moment in history. The main stage props have been put in place. The curtain is about to rise for a prophetic play. How will this drama play out and what role will the Antichrist and his cashless society play? We will look first at the current situation and then to the Scriptures to see what insights they can give us into the immense changes ahead.

2

How Smart is the Smart Card?

A Penny for Your Thoughts

If you have ever driven in the Northeast, you are familiar with toll booths. Though they are never mentioned by travel brochures, which emphasize the fall foliage, visitors had better not try to travel any distance without rolls of nickels, dimes, and quarters. Every few miles you have to slow down as you approach a toll booth and hand your coins to the often less-than-cheerful attendant. Or, if you have the correct change, you can test your hand-eye coordination by tossing your coins into the basket from your car window, praying that you won't be humiliated by missing the mark and having to crawl under the car to retrieve a quarter while honking traffic stacks up behind you.

Good news! It won't be that way in the future. In fact, in some places these monetary transportation sentries are already obsolete. You still pay a toll, but you don't even slow down. From California to Connecticut electronic toll collection systems (ETCs) are under development and in use that automatically read and deduct the toll from a "smart" card and a small transponder attached to your car. This new technology allows you to periodically replenish your smart toll card and keep on moving. All of this is just the beginning of a greater nationwide plan called Intelligent Transportation Systems (ITS). Not only will you watch the road, the road will soon watch you![1]

"Okay, What Is It?"

Have you renewed your driver's license lately? If so, perhaps you had your fingerprint recorded electronically. What about the last time you used an ATM machine? What type of card was used, and what information was on the card? Was it an ATM card only, or a debit card, or perhaps the new smart card? Thanks to new trends in debit cards, smart cards, and credit cards, soon your driver's license may not be the only card displaying your photograph.

The latest wrinkle in personal technology is the "smart card," for which a major promotional campaign was developed to coincide with the 1996 Summer Olympics in Atlanta. It is a cash substitute which looks like a credit card but is preloaded with money or information. When you make a purchase, the amount of the sale is simply deducted from the balance stored on the tiny microchip on the card. This microchip enables the card to store more information and perform more functions than the magnetic-stripe card. New in the United States, smart cards are probably best-known in France, where they are widely used as telephone cards and can be purchased at any newspaper stand or post office. In the United States, the Olympic campaign

> signals the start of a major trend, with sponsors planning to introduce cards in more cities after the Olympics. This fall, for example, Chase Manhattan and Citibank plan to offer Visa and MasterCard smart cards for use at 500 New York City locations. "Most Americans will have a smart card in their pocket by the year 2001," predicts Bill Barr, vice president of the Smart Card Forum, a consortium of banks, credit-card companies and technology firms.[2]

Smart Card: Don't Shop Without It

The cover of the November 3, 1995 edition of *Asia Week* magazine reads, "Smart Move? The Card That Could Rule Our Lives." Inside the magazine, several extensive articles discuss the rise of smart cards and the demise of currency in Asia. A recent *USA Today* survey noted:

> Technology may soon deliver to our wallets "smart cards"—pre-paid payment cards with computer chips that indicate credit for a specific amount of money. And if such cards become reality, consumers are ready. Asked if or how they would use them, more than half of shoppers said they would use them and most knew exactly how the cards would be used.[3]

More than 50 percent of those surveyed by *USA Today* indicated they would use the card on necessities such as gasoline and groceries.[4] The combination of smart-card technology and computer on-line shopping appeals to many consumers. Smart Food Co-op—a Cambridge, Massachusetts, service—now offers customers the opportunity to shop for groceries on-line via the Internet. While there are some problems still to be overcome, experts predict that more than 25 percent of U.S. consumers will shop this way by the turn of the century.[5]

Author Steven Levy is certain that technology is taking us in the direction described above:

> The next great leap of the digital age is, quite literally, going to hit you in the wallet. Those dollar bills you fold up and stash away are headed, with inexorable certainty, toward cryptographically sealed digital streams, stored on a microchip-loaded "smart card" (a plastic card with a microchip), a palm-sized "electronic wallet" (a calculator-sized reader and loader for those cards), or the hard disk of your computer, wired for buying sprees at the virtual mall.[6]

There is much more of this technology available and being used than you probably think. Visa, MasterCard, and AT&T are among the U.S. corporations currently marketing smart cards. AT&T has licensed its smart-card technology, and it is being used by at least one airline (for ticketless boarding), for highway toll-collection in Italy and in this country, and by a cashless vending machine company in the United States and Europe.[7] In Europe and Asia there are a host of other companies using smart cards. The *AsiaWeek* article notes that because of the new smart cards, the way thousands of Asians live, work, and spend will never be the same again. Indeed, one smart-card technology consultant believes that Asians will own at least a third of the more than one billion chip-based cards he expects will be in circulation by 2000.[8]

"Who Is Using Them Now?"

Will smart cards really catch on? The industry giants think so. John Bermingham, president of AT&T Smart Cards, stated:

> Our society is clearly moving towards an era when cash is no longer the most common form of payment. Smart cards will be the standard currency of this cashless society. Just as credit cards have replaced cash for large-value transactions in many parts of the world over the last 30 years, smart cards are likely to replace cash for many smaller transactions.[9]

What kind of small transactions can they be used for? You name it, and it's probably being developed. Smart cards are already in use in conjunction with:

Cash registers	Video arcades
Newspaper boxes	Supermarkets
Parking gates	Fast-food services
Parking meters	Pay phones
Vending machines	Turnstiles
Laundromats	Service stations
Photocopiers	Mass transit systems
Fax machines	Correctional facilities

The list goes on and on. Should we avoid using these services? Not necessarily. None of these uses is inherently bad. Instead, the use of smart-card technology is very convenient. The issue isn't to "beware," but to "be aware." We need to understand what is going on in the world in which we live and consider the implications. The smart card is here, its use is growing, and we will at some point interact with it if we haven't already.

Below is a list of a few of the nations currently using smart-card technology and how they are employing it:

- United States—Visa unveiled its new card for the 1996 Summer Olympics, which is to be used at more than 5000 Atlanta area sites. Other uses include cashless vending machines and special pay phones.
- Italy—Highway toll collection.
- England—Vending machines and cards translate one currency into another.
- China—Test cards on Hainan Island record social service benefits. In Beijing some electricity meters are activated by prepaid cards.
- Hong Kong—Cards reward bonus dollars immediately upon purchase.
- Japan—More than 11 million cards in use. One company uses the cards to serve as both credit cards and keys to company facilities.
- Philippines—One credit-card company uses cards as an installment card for low-income users.
- Singapore—Tourist cards are being tested to eliminate money changers. Plans are being formulated for a civil-service card that records medical claims, administers payments, and opens doors.
- Thailand—Some ATM cards can be used to obtain health and emergency services.

• Belgium—More than 50,000 cards are in use for daily small purchases.

• Mexico—Cards can be used instead of traveler's checks at some locations.

These examples are only a portion of the worldwide use of smart cards. And their uses are rapidly expanding to immigration cards, passports, driver's licenses, health cards, insurance cards, voter registration cards, ID badges, phone cards, and welfare cards. In China, cards may be part of a television security system (censorship) that allows selected officials the opportunity to preview international programs before they are transmitted to the larger population.[10] Because of their convenience, the popularity of the smart card is growing rapidly.

Every country in the world either is, or will be, involved with smart cards at some level. The development of smart technology by one country compels others to follow, since a great deal of the interaction between nations involves technology.

We can see the way this works in the United States. Some readers may remember what is was like before their homes had a telephone. Obviously, you couldn't call someone who did not have a phone. Many people acquired telephones simply to accommodate those wishing to contact them by phone. The same is true today on a larger level as technology soars forward. Many people have acquired fax machines, pagers, cellular phones, and home computers because "it is the way people communicate now." This creates demand, and before long everyone feels the pressure to upgrade to the latest device.

A similar dynamic is fueling the development of cashless technology in every country of the globe. Every country has to be involved in some level of smart technology, at least for purposes of banking and telecommunications, in order to remain competitive in a global market. In fact, some undeveloped countries are leaping to a higher overall level of technology because when they do incorporate technology, they jump in at the newest level without having to transition out of older technology. In other words, they move right to the head of the line.

Only One Card?

With so much interest in smart-card technology, most people will probably initially carry more than one card. AT&T, Mondex, Hughes, Motorola, Visa, MasterCard, Bankard, Nippon Telegraph and Telephone, and a host of other companies may be reluctant to go to a single card. The competition and potential economic gain of having many cards is simply too great. Customers are also reluctant to carry only one card. A survey done by the Smart Card Forum found only one in five respondents favored a single card that carried all the possible uses.[11] A unified technology? Yes. A single card? Not so fast. At least not without enormous changes. But there is a card under development which will eliminate the need for several others you now possess.

A National ID Card?

Open your purse or wallet and pull out the small stack of cards you carry daily. You probably have a driver's license, an insurance card for health services, some credit cards (too many), maybe a military or an employment ID, perhaps a Social Security card, a library card, possibly an immigration card, and some business cards. That's quite a stack! Let's take about half of them and combine them into one card, and combine the other half in a second card. Put the financial cards in one pile and the others in a second pile—one for bucks and one for bureaucracy! The first one we'll call a smart card, and we have already seen how smart cards are being used. The second one we'll call a national identity card.

The idea of a national identity card in the United States and elsewhere has been proposed, and as with everything else we have discussed, is met with both glee and gloom. The issues that ignite conversation are usually those concerning illegal immigration and crime. Proponents believe that a national identification card would help control these social problems. But opponents remind us about the concerns of privacy and excessive government control. This debate will certainly continue. The idea is not as popular in the United States as it is elsewhere. One British survey reportedly showed an approval rating of nearly 75 percent.[12] Economist Thomas Sowell has it right when he argues that "most Americans probably have no more objection in principle to a national identity card than to some form of gun control. It is only in practice that we know it will never stop there."[13]

Get Smart!

Smart cards aren't the only smart things in the present or the future. Many other "smart" products are beginning to revolutionize various aspects of society. Among the items are:

- Smart clothes—Chips used on clothes reveal when and where the item was manufactured, when it was imported, and when it went on the rack, and have the potential of adding information on the purchaser and cost
- Smart houses—Some have pantries that track groceries as they are used and utilities that can be controlled by phone
- Smart roads—Roadbeds monitor weather conditions and issue warnings for motorists
- Smart cars—Maps and directions broadcast via global positioning satellites
- Smart tires—Logging trucks with computers linked to satellites gain road and weather condition information and automatically adjust air pressure in the tires
- Smart pucks—Hockey pucks containing a microchip transmit data to network computers
- Smart radios and TVs—Interactive and personalized electronics allow you to respond to commercials or adjust programming
- Smart telephones—Phones with built-in answering machines, faxes, caller ID, and phones that combine all known communication functions at once while also offering mobility[14]

If you ever fumble through your wallet or pocketbook looking for the right card or try to cash a check with a clerk who wants to see a driver's license and one or two other pieces of identification, you understand how compelling the ease of a single card is. But as the old saying goes, do you really want to put "all your eggs in one basket"? And is there cause for legitimate concern?

3

"Brother, Can You Spare a Dime?"

DIGITAL DOLLARS
AND ELECTRONIC MONEY

J im and Gary were driving around Nashville on the lookout, as always, for good deals on musical instruments. In a dusty shop on a back street, the owner smiled at their inquiry and disappeared into the back room. He emerged with a vintage Martin guitar. "Isn't she a beauty?" he intoned. Gary's jaw dropped. He had been looking for years for just such a guitar. When the man told him the price, his heart skipped a beat. A bargain. "I'll take it," he said. But when he opened his wallet, he remembered he'd spent his last dollars on dinner last night. He looked hopefully at Jim.

Well, what are good friends for? Jim said. He had his transfer terminal with him and more than enough funds to cover the purchase.

"How about it, Jim? A loan for just a few days, okay?"

"Yeah, I guess so—as long as it's not a habit."

Jim keyed in the amount of the guitar and swiped his card through the terminal slot. Then Gary swiped his card though and Jim struck the "transfer key." In a matter of microseconds the funds were transferred from Jim's account and Gary was the owner of the guitar of his dreams. The following week when the funds were available to Gary, they met for lunch and, just as simply as before, swiped their cards through the terminal to repay Jim's account.

Transactions like the one Jim and Gary made could be commonplace in the near future. Like electronic banking today, personal money would change accounts without physically changing hands.

Shop 'Til You Drop

The growing use of computer technology, the Internet, and the phenomenal amount of information available is not only changing the way many people work and communicate, it's also changing the way people shop. Why shop at the mall when you can shop at home at a worldwide electronic mall that never closes? As one article in an international publication said:

> Imagine a vast shopping mall open every day, 24 hours a day. The shelves are stacked high with goods from all over the world. Rude salespeople have been banished and crowds are non-existent. Now imagine that mall peopled with con artists as well as customers, thieves as well as merchants. You are beginning to have an idea of the challenge facing those who want the Internet to be the biggest boon for business since money was invented.[1]

Making the Internet both shopper-friendly and financially secure is a growing desire among merchants. One important step toward satisfying this desire for security is the continuing development of electronic money.

The Buck Stops Here

Until recently, one of the problems connected with shopping through the use of personal computers and the Internet was credit-card security. In the same way that a thief can peer over the shoulder of an unsuspecting pay-phone user to steal a phone-card number, a hacker can easily scan the Internet to steal a credit-card number as it is being passed from a consumer to a merchant. To provide security against this threat, financial transactions have been handled by means external to the Internet. An article in *The Economist* described this difficulty:

> Customers, browsing ("net surfing") at their computers, can trawl through these electronic shops viewing products, reading descriptions and sometimes trying samples. What they lack is the means to buy from their keyboard, on impulse. They could pay by credit card, transmitting the necessary data by modem; but intercepting messages on the Internet is trivially easy for a smart hacker, so sending a credit-card number in an unscrambled message is inviting trouble. It would be relatively safe to send a credit-card number encrypted with a hard-to-break code; but that would require either a general adoption across the Internet of standard encoding protocols (which might happen, but has

not done so yet), or the making of prior ad hoc arrangements between buyer and sellers.[2]

Such concerns are now being addressed, thanks to the advent of electronic money.

"Now that it is acquiring a more commercial character, the race to develop and market a form of electronic money that will be as fast, flexible and global as the Internet itself has become one of the hottest topics in the computer industry."[3]

The electronic transfer of funds is not new. Such transfers have been a standard for years in the banking industry. However, the potential of bringing similar technology into private homes and personal transactions makes the transfer of electronic money even more appealing. Today a number of companies are working on the concept of electronic money, finding ways to market it and even bank it. The Internet provides a huge forum for such experimentation:

> The Internet is that rare thing, a vast market visibly hungry for a fairly well-defined product. As such, it is proving to be a tremendous forcing-ground for ideas and experiments that, if they succeed, will have implications extending far beyond the Internet itself.... The convergence of money, commerce and personal computers represents one of the great new markets of modern times.[4]

With so much potential, the race is on, and there are plenty of contestants. Electronic money is here to stay, and may soon make cash and coins an endangered species.

It Doesn't Jingle—It Blips

Authors Daniel C. Lynch and Leslie Lundquist have called digital money "the cuneiform of a new age."[5] They offer the following hypothetical but helpful scenario to introduce the concept of digital money:

> Using digital money, lobbyist Alice can transfer money to Senator Bob so that newspaper reporter Eve cannot determine who contributed the funds. Bob can deposit Alice's money in his campaign account, even though the bank has no idea who Alice is. But if Alice uses the same piece of digital money to bribe two different members of Congress, the bank can detect that. And if Congressman Bob tries to deposit Alice's contribution into two different accounts, the banks can detect that too.[6]

From this scenario, Lynch and Lundquist present six properties or principles of an ideal digital-money system:

1. Independence: The security of digital money must not depend on its existence in any singular physical location.

2. Security: Digital money must not be reusable. That is, it must not be possible to spend the same digital money more than once. Thus Alice cannot bribe two different Congressmen with the same piece of digital money.

3. Privacy (Untraceability): Digital money must protect the privacy of its users. It must not, of itself, allow for tracing the relationship between a person and a purchase. Thus, lobbyist Alice can transfer campaign funds to Congressman Bob and the bank will not know the identity of the contributor.

4. Off-line Payment: Merchants who accept digital money must not depend on a connection to a network so that a transaction can be made. Alice could transfer digital money to Congressman Bob simply by plugging in her smart card to his computer; the digital money is independent of the means transporting it.

5. Transferability: Digital money must be transferable to others. When Alice transfers digital money to Congressman Bob, her identity is completely removed from the money.

6. Divisibility: A quantity of digital money must be divisible into smaller amounts, and they must total up again when recombined. If Alice transfers 100 digital pennies to Congressman Bob, he gets a digital $1.00.[7]

These are the general principles that companies involved in the development of digital cash are currently pursuing. It's a high goal, but there has been some success.

On-line currency has as many names as the companies promoting it, and often the names are the same as those companies. There's digital cash, NetBill, NetCheque, electronic money, e-money, NetCash, CyberBucks, e-cash, CyberCash, DigiCash, NetBank, Mondex, electronic cash, First Virtual, and more. Regardless of the company or the name, each one desires to attract new consumers. You may have "on-line pocket change," but you won't have the jingle in your pocket anymore.

Microsoft founder Bill Gates looks to a time when a wallet-sized personal computer will replace cash:

> Rather than holding paper currency, the new wallet will store unforgettable digital money. Today when you hand someone a dollar bill, check, gift

certificate, or other negotiable instrument, the transfer of paper represents a transfer of funds. But money does not have to be expressed on paper. Credit card charges and wired funds are exchanges of digital financial information. Tomorrow the wallet PC will make it easy for anyone to spend and accept digital funds. Your wallet will link into a store's computer to allow money to be transferred without any physical exchange at a cash register. Digital cash will be used in interpersonal transactions too. If your son needs money, you might digitally slip five bucks from your wallet PC to his.[8]

Such money may not feel the same as cash, sound the same as cash, or look the same as cash, but many people are "banking" on the hope that it will spend the same.

Is It Really That Easy?

Will shopping on the Internet or loaning someone money really be such an easy transaction? Probably so, even though it might be hard to imagine. Almost every type of cash transaction performed today can be duplicated electronically. There are exceptions, but they are few. In a cashless society that uses digital dollars, electronic terminals similar to the ones we now swipe our credit cards or ATM cards through would continue to be a necessity. David Warwick writes of these terminals:

> Under the new money system, terminals would be developed for use in noncommercial personal transactions. Some would be placed in common locations like public telephones for anyone to use.

Privately owned models would be small enough to
carry in a pocket or purse.[9]

There's no question but that this is the direction we are
headed. It is simply a matter of time and of overcoming the
initial glitches and fears.

Cybereconomics 101

Perhaps somewhere in your educational background you
took a course in economics, microeconomics, or macroeco-
nomics. Economics has its own terminology, equations, theo-
ries, and models. Like all academic disciplines and professions,
it is a world unto itself. Into this world has now come another
world: cyberspace. The merging (some would say "collision")
of these two worlds has created new challenges for professional
economists, as well as the public and private sectors.

Computer technology has reaped enormous financial
rewards for many people, and has changed the lives of all
of us.

Why Electronic Cash?

Why use electronic cash? Proponents usually give three
reasons: versatility, security, and privacy. DigiCash, one of
the leaders and founders of electronic money, makes the following comments in its promotional literature:

> The security provided by electronic cash is unmatched
> in scope and cost-effectiveness. There's no need for an
> acquirer of value to contact a central system more than
> weekly, because the terminology is secure against cheating
> and misuse even without on-line connections. Since elec-
> tronic cash is digitally "signed" by the issuer, there's no

room for dispute over payments, and no mutually trusted center is necessary. All parties need only select and protect their own hardware. . . . Electronic cash, unlike even paper cash, is unconditionally untraceable. The "blinding" carried out by the user's own device makes it impossible for anyone to link payment to payer. But users can prove unequivocally that they did or did not make a particular payment, without revealing anything more. Besides appealing to consumers, this level of privacy limits exposure to future data-privacy legislation and reduces record-keeping costs.[10]

This certainly sounds secure and private, but these are the words of an advocate. The founder of DigiCash, David Chaum, is extremely serious about the issue of privacy,[11] but is it really possible that electronic money is "unconditionally untraceable"? Not everyone is so sure:

Hard cash, of course, is anonymous—you can spend your printed bills with the assurance that no one can trace your expenditures or compile a dossier on your lifetime spending records. But electronic cash has no such assurances. Its computer-mediated nature makes traceability the course of least resistance. This gives rise to a provocative question: Can digital cash become anonymous, as real-world money is? And if so, should it be?[12]

This question of principle of privacy or untraceability is the most vexing question facing digital money.

How Does It Work?

There are several methods for handling electronic money. One is to have electronic money in an account at an electronic bank. The buyer can authorize the bank to make charges against a credit card. The buyer simply orders items on the Internet and provides the seller with his account number at the bank. The bank sends an e-mail message to the customer asking them to confirm the purchase. Once confirmed, the customer's conventional credit card is charged. This method is a low-level type of electronic money that primarily protects against credit card fraud. It is basic, entry-level electronic economics.[13] But experts believe it holds little short-term promise:

> This may be a good way to provoke interest in electronic commerce and pander to Internet users' appetite for novelty. But few sellers will want to deal routinely on trust, and few buyers will have the means or the desire to verify possibly hundreds of small transactions each day or week.[14]

A second model for handling digital cash is that of electronic money-tokens, which contain a prepaid amount of money available for use. The concept is similar to prepaid telephone smart cards or public transportation cards.

> What travels from buyer to seller is not merely information that will enable them to settle a transaction subsequently by other means, but something much closer to money itself—a proxy, as it were, for the money with which the card was purchased.[15]

The problem with this method is that of verification and forgery. Is the payment real or a digital forgery?

Because of forgery and privacy concerns, a third model has been created. It uses a hidden "signature" that provides security for the owner and electronic certainty for the seller:

> Since digital forgeries are, by definition, perfect copies (two identical strings of numbers are two identical strings of numbers), the only way to make such electronic money trustworthy would be to build into it at the time of its creation a hidden "signature" (think of the watermark in a banknote) that would establish it as a bona-fide product of its issuer and at the same time give it a unique identity (like the number on a banknote). Then, even if a unit of electronic money were to be copied, it could still be spent once only; the recipient would check the signature with the issuer, and the issuer would detect the duplication.[16]

It is this model that DigiCash is working to produce. They believe it is safe, secure, and private. Anonymity is a foundational concept in creation of digital money, and such money is convenient because it can be created in any denomination.

Chaos in Cyberspace

The phenomenal growth of the Internet is pressing the concept of digital money forward. Steven Levy writes:

> Cyberspace is destined to be the first battleground of the digital money wars. While it will take years, perhaps decades for e-money to replace hard

currency in the physical world, the virtual world not only can't accommodate the current system, but is desperate for immediate implementation of the digital equivalent. Everyone agrees that the Internet is the staging ground for the first true boom in electronic commerce, but it's a transactional wasteland. You can't buy anything without a credit card. You can't even collect on a $2 bet with a friend.[17]

On a micro level, security and some certainty of transfer may exist for an individual's transactions, but on a macro level, it still does not exist.

The financial world is a complex and chaotic one. So also is the world of computer technology. What happens globally when the two merge?

As the electronic economy takes shape, it must accommodate conflicting and often contradictory forces—forces that no one completely understands. It is a new world based on information, but information is always shifting, going out of date, being revised, updated, and amended. Information is often pregnant with what can only be called insults to stability.

The new world is one in which localism—local markets, currencies, and rules—must contend with globalism. It is a world where governments have less power and the private sector more, where governments participate in markets—by borrowing money—but can no longer control them.[18]

What Kurtzman says is certainly true today, but will it be true tomorrow, or will the chaos change that too? When it works, it works. But what happens when it doesn't work?

A Penny for Your Thoughts

It seems clear that electronic money and the cashless system offer us convenience and speed. Though there continue to be security concerns, the electronic transfer system as it exists works well. Banks have been using electronic transfers for years, and normally there are few major problems. In fact, every day 14,000 American banks electronically transfer about 2.1 trillion dollars over their networks. "In a day enough money goes from bank to bank to cover the salaries of about 100 million working Americans for a year, to pay for seven years of defense spending, to neutralize seven years of balance-of-trade deficits, or to reduce the national debt by half."[19]

The Wall Street Journal, industry journals, weekly magazines, financial newsletters, and a host of other materials can give us valuable insights into the current economic and cultural trends of our nation and the world. However, sometimes we would do well to read history. Kingdoms, empires, nations, and dynasties blow across the pages of history like Texas tumbleweeds. They rise and they fall for many reasons: some economic, some diplomatic, some military, and some spiritual. The perceptive person will read and evaluate history and current events and many other sources of knowledge as he or she plans for the future. One of them should be the prophetic literature of the Bible, for in its pages is found not only wisdom, but also truth.

4

Facts, Fear, and Fascination

THE TRUTH ABOUT THE CASHLESS SOCIETY

W hat are the implications of a cashless society for our lives? Is it a time-saver or a trap, a help or a hindrance? It's definitely the wave of the future. But are we going to ride on it or have it come crashing down upon us?

The concept of a cashless society has been advanced in the United States for more than 25 years.[1] Even in the nineteenth century some philosophers speculated about a utopian world where money would be replaced by a card based upon an individual's credit. Until recently, its meaning and supporting concepts were known in the field of economics and to sociologists looking to the future, but it was not commonly used in the media or in daily conversations. However, all of that is quickly changing, for its use is increasing daily. This is because the technology supporting the concept of a cashless society has grown exponentially in the last few years.

Economic historian Glyn Davies has noted that although there have been many minor technical improvements in the medium of exchange (money) in the last 1000 years, there have only been two major improvements:

> The first at the end of the Middle Ages when the printing of money began to supplement the minting of coins, and the second in our own time when electronic money transfer was invented.... The first stimulated the rise of banking, while the second is opening the way towards universal and instantaneous money transfer in the global village of the twenty-first century.[2]

If Davies's observations are correct, then contemporary society is experiencing a remarkable shift in the field of economics and in the way daily "bread and butter" transactions are made. So what then is the cashless society?

"The Dictionary, Please!"

As we have noted, in the strictest sense a cashless society would be one in which *no* forms of currency exist. All coins, paper money, checks, stocks, bonds, and other economic representations of personal wealth would be eliminated. The sounds of change rattling in pockets or crisp bills being counted would be replaced by the electronic pulses of computers sending economic information around the globe almost instantaneously through a worldwide network. Just as many people today have "direct deposit" for their paychecks, automatic debit for the payment of some bills, or on-line financial programs to pay other bills, so in the future *all* financial transactions, it is claimed, will be made by electronic transfer. It is not the eradication of personal wealth, but a drastic change in how that wealth is represented and in how financial transactions are accomplished. One computer engineer has noted,

> With the technology that is available today we are on the threshold of the total elimination of cash as we know it. This evolution to a new system will be very gradual, but nevertheless, culminate in a society without the tangible currency in use today. It is the inevitable next step in the exchange of goods and services.[3]

What are we to think of such statements? If it is true, there are consequences that reach beyond the realm of economics into the realms of politics, psychology, and sociology. We are left to ponder the important moral, ethical, and theological implications of such a change.

Money serves two primary functions in society: first, as a medium of exchange and second, as an indication of wealth. In the cashless society, cash will simply become electronically transferable credit in units of "dollars." The word dollar will itself have little significance other than to refer to the "virtual cash" or "cybercash" that a person has in his or her account in a large data bank.[4] Electronic cash transactions are fast and inexpensive; however, it is money's second function, as an indication of wealth or value, that is slowing down the development of the cashless society since electronic money isn't tangible, and, therefore, there is a reluctance by some people to use it. But such obstacles to a cashless society are being addressed and gradually overcome—indeed, so much so that in 1995 the world's first trans-electronic bank opened its "virtual doors." Advertising from this institution summarizes the economic direction in which society is moving:

> Ideally, the ultimate e-cash [electronic cash] will be a currency without a country (or a currency of all countries), infinitely exchangeable without the expense and inconvenience of conversion between local denominations. It may constitute itself as a wholly new currency with its own denomination the "cyberdollar," perhaps.... It is hard to imagine that the existence of an international, easy-to-use, cheap-to-process, hard-to-tax electronic money will not then force freer convertibility on traditional currencies.... A wild vision, perhaps; but most people would have said the same in 1970 if somebody had guessed that within 25 years millions of people would regard themselves as part-time citizens of something they called cyberspace. It is surely not surprising that they should now want to take some spending money when they go there.[5]

As Steven Levy, an author and fellow at the Freedom Forum Media Studies Center, has written, "The killer application for electronic networks isn't video-on-demand. It's going to hit you where it really matters—in your wallet. Digital cash, e-money, bit bucks . . . whatever you call it, not only will it revolutionize the Net [Internet], it will change the global economy."[6]

While much of this information may be new for us or sound too futuristic for us to be concerned with now, such is not the case. Although headlines do not focus on the cashless society and its supporting technology, there is ample literature and advertising regarding it. Once you start looking for it, the evidence and documentation is abundant. An afternoon search on the Internet provided the authors with hundreds of pages of articles and advertisements that are less than two years old!

Where Have All the Dollars Gone?

"Few people realize that money, in the traditional sense, has met its demise. Fewer still have paused to reflect on the implications of that fact."[7] With these astonishing words, Joel Kurtzman, executive editor of the *Harvard Business Review*, succinctly states the truth about a little-known but international reality:

> Money has been transmogrified. It is no longer a *thing*, an object you can dig up at the beach or search for behind the cushions of a sofa; it is a *system*. Money is a network that comprises hundreds of thousands of computers of every type, wired together in places as lofty as the Federal Reserve— which settles accounts between banks every night that are worth trillions of dollars—and as mundane as the thousands of gas pumps around the world outfitted to take credit and debit cards. The network of money includes all the world's markets—stock, bond, futures, currency, interest rate, options, and so on.[8]

So how much does all of this affect us? The answer is, "More than you think," for while we may not give much thought to the larger world beyond our homes and families, or our jobs and communities, we are economically linked to the entire world. We live on a microeconomic level, but we are part of the global macroeconomic system, whether we know it or not. Technology is shrinking the globe to the point that Disney's song seems prophetic: "It's a small world after all."

A Global Economy Here and Now

What do London, Tokyo, and New York have in common? Money. Today, all the world's markets are linked together. The economic fortunes and misfortunes of individual countries such as Japan, France, Mexico, or Canada have international repercussions that affect the finance and industry of the entire world. From an economic perspective, nations do not rise or fall alone. "In reality ... we are all on the megabyte standard."[9] Not only are the effects of national economies felt worldwide, they are also known and experienced almost instantaneously because of current technology. An economic eruption or disturbance in New York sends financial shock waves throughout the globe. The economic scene is highly complex, technologically integrated, and extremely unstable.

Kurtzman continues:

> Millions of computers threaded together through tens of millions of miles of cable make up the neural network of money. That complex system resembles a snowflake, an elaborate fiber-optic pattern of connections with nothing at the center. It is complicated, complex, and, paradoxically, both strong and fragile.[10]

The increasing complexity of the international economic system and its reliance upon technology makes it highly susceptible to minor and major disruptions. With the use of computers, everyone from stockbrokers to banks to private citizens can trade stocks, bonds, commodities, and transfer money with the click of a button. Edward Cornish, president of the World Future Society and editor of *The Futurist*, describes the monetary opportunities of life in the next few decades: "Electronic banking will become increasingly global, which means that people should find it easy to keep their money in different countries and currencies."[11] He illustrates this belief: "For example, a Canadian may have an account denominated in German marks at a Cayman Islands bank. Individuals may constantly switch their money about the world in search of better interest or exchange rates—or to evade taxes. The result may be an increasingly unstable world financial system."[12]

How Much, How Soon?

Is the cashless system really catching on in our society, or is it a passing fad? The fields of economics and technology are fast-paced arenas where both statistics and products are soon outdated, but the indisputable fact is that in the last few years there has been a significant increase in electronic, or cashless, transactions. Every day in New York City, "more than $1.9-trillion electronically changes hands at nearly the speed of light. These dollars—and the cares, hopes, and fears they represent—appear as momentary flashes on a screen."[13] That's a lot of money. In 1993, electronic transfers in the United States accounted for 18 percent of the 55 trillion dollars spent by government, consumers, and corporations. This represented a 200 percent increase since 1986, during which time the number of check and cash transactions rose only 17 percent. As of 1994, 20 percent of utility bills, 16 percent of automobile loans, and 17 percent of mortgage payments were paid electronically.[14] Additionally, in 1994 more than a third of all U.S. workers were on direct deposit of their paychecks, as opposed to eight percent in 1988. Each year almost half of the federal government's budget is transferred electronically.[15]

Credit cards are another example of how the trend toward a cashless society has become big business. While only about 15 percent of retail sales are made with credit cards, this number is rising. More people will be forced to use credit cards as the use of cash for handling transactions gradually disappears. Credit card companies are trying hard to capitalize on this opportunity. "We've got to be better than cash and checks," said a Visa International official.[16] The statistics on credit card use are staggering. For example, Visa, the largest credit card company, has 300 million cards out and comprises half the credit card market. MasterCard has about 27 percent of the credit card market, and American Express has about 20 percent. Visa's worldwide network includes 20,000 banks and 10 million merchants in 247 countries. This vast system handles more than 500 billion dollars a year in credit card transactions.[17]

Eighty percent of Americans regularly use credit cards.[18] As technology develops and newer, faster, and safer means of electronic transactions are developed, the percentage may grow and the number of personal transactions by individuals will increase. Just as we communicate more by phone than by letter, so will our financial transactions be more by electronic means than by cash or check.

Think about your own financial transactions:

- Do you use direct deposit for your paycheck?
- Do you have automatic withdrawl from your account for house payments, car payments, life insurance, or other monthy expenditures?
- How many credit cards do you use regularly?
- How much cash do you usually carry in your purse, pocket, or wallet?
- Have you used a credit card to pay for groceries?
- Have you purchased gasoline with a credit card?
- Do you have a debit card?
- How often do you use an automatic teller machine?
- How often do you give out your credit card number over the phone to buy merchandise?
- Do you use a personal computer for any of your financial transactions?

Many of us probably participate in several, if not all, of the activities above on a fairly regular basis. Cashless transactions are convenient, and they relieve us carrying large sums of cash. There is nothing inherently wrong or evil about using this technology. However, the activities above move us toward a cashless society. We are already participating in its early stages. If we are going to interact with contemporary society and live and work in it, then we must responsibly and critically face the issues that are part of it. Many of those issues deal with the proper use of technology and its role in our lives. The issues and questions surrounding a cashless society are not so much the issues of *when* to use the technology, but of *how much* to use it.

Megabyte Money

The entire concept of economics and the monetary units of which it speaks have changed. "Cold cash" is being replaced by "megabyte money." Joel Kurtzman writes in *The Death of Money*:

> For the last twenty years or so, the world and its economy have been in the midst of a wrenching change. What has changed? Money. Not the dollars in our pockets or the coins in our hands. That money—tangible money, old fashioned money—now accounts for only the tiniest fraction of all the money that is in circulation around the world today. It is a phantom form from the past, an anachronism. In its place, traveling the world incessantly without rest and nearly at the speed of light, is an entirely new form of money based not on metal or paper but on technology, mathematics, and science. And like Einstein's assumption that a photon of light creates the universe wherever it goes, this new "megabyte" money is creating a new and different world wherever it proceeds.[19]

Money was once stored in vaults or under mattresses. It was accounted for in large ledgers in black and red ink. It was backed by gold and silver. It was usually accumulated slowly and through hard work and perseverance. But much of that has changed.

> Money now is an image. Simultaneously, it can be displayed on millions of computer screens on millions of desks around the world. But in reality it is located nowhere and needs no vault for safekeeping.

Yet, while money has no real location, it has created an environment that is paradoxically everywhere while taking up no physical space.[20]

On an international level and from a macroeconomic perspective, the new money systems and technologies will significantly influence the way nations interact with each other and with their citizens. National boundaries will become far less important, and national economic policies will no longer carry the authority they have in the past.[21]

Another Benefit—Safety

Futurist David R. Warwick envisions a national electronic-money system that would function as a debit-card system. Bank debit cards, as well as the more popular credit cards, are already being used by many individuals, but Warwick foresees a national system on the economic horizon:

> Unlike credit-card systems, in which funds are in effect loaned by banks to card holders, credit would not be involved in the government money system. Each individual's "money" would be held in his money-system account. A transaction would effect an instant transfer of "money" from his account to that of another account holder.[22]

Warwick's model is only one of the types being discussed, and his motivation for such a system is the desire to see a reduction in crime. Such a system, he argues, would reduce many of the crimes that are economically driven. "It does not require lengthy research and analysis to comprehend the principal benefit of adopting electronic money—that once cash is removed from circulation, every crime requiring it would become impossible to perpetrate."[23] His proposed national electronic-money system differs from commercial bank card systems in four areas:

- The money system would be federally operated rather than commercially operated.
- Electronic payment would constitute "legal tender."
- Participants in the system would be able to receive funds as well as pay out funds from their accounts.
- Funds would be transferable between private individuals as well as between merchants and individuals.[24]

Such a system appeals to many prospective users because it does not eradicate other means of financial transactions, only cash. Checks, money orders, traveler's checks, cashier's checks, and letters of credit would all still be utilized in the marketplace. Only cash would be eliminated, being supplanted by electronic money. Cashless systems such as credit cards and automatic teller machines would not necessarily change, with the exception that you could no longer obtain cash from the ATM.

All of the proposed cashless models have benefits and disadvantages, but it is easy to envision such a model in the not-too-distant future.

All for One and One for All!

Will the cashless system mean universal participation? Will everyone be *required* to be a part of it? The answers are yes and no. The initial shift will be gradual (just as with direct deposit, use of ATM machines, etc.), but as more and more people use it, it will become standard practice. It will not be forced on the majority of people any more than people are "forced" to use computers, checks, or credit cards today, but it will simply become the most convenient and perhaps prudent way to transact business.

A Warning

In our present society, technology is not being directly used to control people, and research and development is exploding and seemingly giving more freedom to individuals. However, this could change rapidly. Currently, the development of technology allows for specialization. It promotes diversification and the decentralization of power. Yet it is possible to conceive of the development and implementation of "technological choke points" or "information locks" which would control access to the flood of information and activity and have the capability of excluding individuals or groups from participation. Just as the locks in a canal control the level and flow of water, as well as permitting or restricting shipping through it, the same could become true in cyberspace. Some people might voluntarily exclude themselves from participation; others might involuntarily be excluded.

Participation in the future cashless society *may* be as neutral as it is today, to the extent that we already use it. But it also has the potential of being used for evil. The possibility of misuse concerns us, because there may be little or no choice of future participation in the cashless society; it could easily turn socially sour and become a design of "participate or perish."

Albert Borgmann, a professor of philosophy at the University of Montana, has written that "technology is among the most important and confused topics in the national conversation. It rarely appears on the official agenda, yet it is at issue in all significant debates."[25] What is true on a national level is true on a personal level. We must strive daily to understand the foundation of our beliefs and actions. What we do publicly and privately and the values we hold have tremendous consequences. There is truly "a world of difference" between a Christian and a non-Christian worldview. The purpose and role of technology is a part of every person's worldview. We must ask how new technologies will be used. As philosophy professor Carl Mitchum has astutely observed:

> We do not live in order to make and use technologies; we make and use technologies in order to live—that is, to live one way rather than another. Given our medical, industrial, and computer technologies, we can seek to assess their benefits and risks and to submit them to the principles of justice, or leave them in the hands of amoral market forces. . . . No matter how we decide to treat the environment, no matter what we decide to do with our computers, it will have an ethical, not just a technical, impact on our lives.[26]

In the broadest sense, technology should be viewed as morally neutral. It is the use we make of it in medicine, industry, defense, transportation, engineering, communications, etc. that gives it its moral aspect. The same computers on which these pages were typed could just as easily have been used for unscrupulous hacking into corporate records or for espionage. It is characteristic of a fallen world that those things which God created for good, men and women will use for evil. The ramifications of original sin are as real in technology as they are in theology.

According to biblical prophecy, some day there will arise one who will use any and all means at his disposal in an attempt to thwart the plan of God and to manipulate the masses for his own power and glory. When he does so, the cashless society maybe a means to his end.

5

Prints, Pulses, and Positive Identity

TOMORROW'S TECHNOLOGY TODAY

When you hum "Home on the Range," the images that pass through your mind may be of the campfire at night, the cowboys at roundup, and the wide open spaces where the "buffalo roam." But in today's world, though the buffalo may roam, we still know where they are. Tracking wildlife, pets, livestock, and even fish has become commonplace. Many such creatures no longer have brands, they have biochips. If we can track inanimate objects such as freight and creatures such as sled dogs on the Iditarod, cattle in the pasture, or Daisy Dog the family pet, then why not humans? If we can put chips in chimps, why not in people?

Biometrics Never Has an Identity Crisis!

Biometrics is the study of identifying people through their physical characteristics and behavioral patterns in conjunction with some form of card or technology. The entire field of biometrics is rapidly expanding and is being used in many areas of contemporary society. Electronic fingerprint readers, voice print recognition, hand image scanners, thermograms (thermal face prints), and retinal identification technology (which reads the unique and unalterable retinal pattern of a person's eye) are some of the growing technologies. Such technologies move well beyond the smart cards, so it is not unthinkable that consumers will one day not even need cards at ATMs.

Within the field of biometrics there is a competition to see which type of identification is best. One of these is the "hand recognition" system:

> Hand recognition ID systems are becoming more common in settings from prisons and private condos to computer rooms and college cafeterias. In comparison to other forms of biometric identification including those which use fingerprints, voice recognition and retinal scanning, supporters of ID systems that rely on the uniqueness of users' hands say that such technology is more reliable and user-friendly.[1]

Proponents of thermal face prints are equally enthusiastic about "thermograms." John Burnell, new director for *Automatic I.D. News*, states:

> A "hot" new technology that never forgets a face is the newest form of personal automatic identification. If you're one in a million, there are 5,000 people in the world just like you—except that your

face releases heat in a pattern as unique as your fingerprint. The heat-release pattern can be recorded and analyzed with a new system from Technology Recognition Systems (TRS), which will use the technology to develop highly secure biometric identification systems....

TRS will pursue eight applications during the next five years: access control, computer security, identification credentials, credit card security, communications security, private records and law enforcement support.[2]

Because biometric technology is "mistake proof," it is not surprising that many are enthusiastic about its possible applications.

101 Different Biometric Possibilities

Biometric technology, though very expensive, is fast, convenient, and extremely reliable. It is being employed by private industry and governments around the world. A CNN report on one application of biometric technology in Australia was very positive:

Left your credit card at home? Forgotten your PIN number? Use your finger to make that purchase or draw money. A new scanning device uses a person's finger to make a positive identification, making credit cards, identity cards, passwords and PIN numbers redundant. The technology developed by an Australian company permits someone to identify themselves by pressing their finger against a device which takes a three-dimensional scan of their fingerprint and instantly matches it with a template stored on a computer. Fingerscan inventor John Parselle explained that the scan works by examining the unique ridges and valleys of a person's finger, as well as the flow of blood through the finger.[3]

It may come as a surprise to note the number of ways that biometrics is currently being employed. The "imaging" market is growing, and more and more companies are forming alliances to enter the marketplace. Some of the current applications include:

- Facial features stored on smart cards to enable more security in financial transactions
- Optical memory cards to identify fingerprints for health care and Social Security pensioners
- Finger imaging at ATMs to replace personal identification numbers
- Finger imaging to replace ID cards and passwords
- Finger imaging to support applications for social services
- Hand scanning to verify a person's vein patterns for credit card authorization
- Finger imaging to prevent check-cashing fraud
- Voice-activated telephone cards
- Bar-coded wristband to track prisoners
- Hand scanning to replace ID cards
- Hand scanning for welfare recipients to help detect fraud
- Thermal face-prints to replace ID cards

- Hand scanning to process immigration at some airports
- Voice prints to replace immigrant work cards
- Military ID cards (MARC) used for multiple purposes
- Optical memory cards to store medical records and data

These applications are just a sampling of what is currently being done. There are many other possibilities.

It's Not On You, It's In You!

The applications noted above could be only interim methods. The ultimate biometric tool is the implantable biochip. Radio Frequency Identification (RFID) technology is one of the most fascinating fields in the biometric industry. RFID technology uses a biochip transponder, which is about the size of a grain of rice. It is implanted in either animals or inanimate products, such as automobiles, in order to track their locations. Such uses on animals are now almost commonplace in the United States and Europe.[4] In 1993, Sematech Corporation announced that it had developed a semiconductor with a device width of only 0.35 microns, which is 1/200th of a human hair.[5] The potential also exists to use the technology for corrective medical procedures. A 1994 article in the *Los Angeles Times* noted a new development in human implant possibilities:

> At least 6 million medical devices a year worldwide are surgically implanted in people.... Years later, if a patient visits a doctor because of problems, medical information

such as the manufacturer of the implant or the name of the surgeon may not be available.

No problem, if the patient's implant carries an implant of its own—a microchip on which all relevant information has been encoded. Called Smart Device, the chip, which is about the size of a grain of rice, is manufactured by Hughes Identification Devices, a subsidiary of Hughes Aircraft Co. In the event of complications with an implant, a doctor could retrieve the information from the chip using a "gun" that emits a radio beam. The gun operates in much the same way that decoders in supermarkets decipher bar coding. The information on the chip would also be recorded on a computer-linked global registry.[6]

Edward Cornish, editor of *The Futurist,* believes that within the next three decades biometrics will be commonplace:

A chip implanted somewhere in our bodies might serve as a combination credit card, passport, driver's license, personal diary, and you name it. No longer would we worry about losing our credit cards while traveling. A chip inserted into our bodies might also give us extra mental power.

Ultratiny computers might also provide enough intelligence for microscopic machines that could be injected into our bodies. These nanomachines would perform such tasks as repairing muscle and brain cells so we could enjoy perpetual youth.

Researchers have already found a way to make "molecular computers" out of pieces of DNA, the genetic material found in the cells of every animal and plant. University of Southern California mathematician Leonard Adleman has reported getting his DNA-computer to solve a mathematical puzzle.[7]

While these uses seem all for the good, it is not difficult to imagine other people creating uses far beyond the original intent of the design.

"One Plus One Equals..."

Is there a danger of misuse of such technology? Many believe there is.

Nationally syndicated columnist Martin Anderson, a senior fellow at the Hoover Institution, warns about the prospects of biochip technology:

> [They are] sort of like a technological tattoo, and far more efficacious than the numbers that the Nazis marked indelibly on the inner forearms of concentration camp prisoners.
>
> True, an implanted transponder can't yet hold anywhere near as much material as a smart card. But if the desire is there, larger size implants and tiny microchips could soon increase its data storage capacity.... There is no difference between being forced to carry a microchip in a plastic card in your wallet or in a little pellet in your arm. The principle that Big Brother has the right to track you is inherent in both. The only thing that differentiates the two techniques is a layer of skin.
>
> Once you denigrate the idea of privacy, all kinds of innovative government controls are possible, things that didn't even occur to Aldous Huxley when he wrote his chilling novel "Brave New World."[8]

The combination of a cash-free environment and biometric technology should be a real concern to everyone. There are positives and negatives involved in a cashless society, as well as pros and cons to smart-card technology and biometrics. These breakthroughs can be used for good or for evil. Consider what might happen if they are joined together for evil. Generally, if you can control a person's finances or resources you can control the person. With cash it is not as easy to control someone's finances as it would be with a cashless system. Given the right circumstances, a cashless system could control finances tightly. Link that tight control with positive identification of people and a traceable personal history about them, and you have the framework to create an extremely authoritarian environment. When we read the Bible, we see that such conjectures closely parallel the prophesied future.

6

"That No Man Might Buy or Sell"

BIBLICAL PROPHECY AND THE CASHLESS SOCIETY

And he causes all, the small and the great, and the rich and the poor, and the free men and the slaves, to be given a mark on their right hand, or on their forehead, and he provides that no one should be able to buy or to sell, except the one who has the mark, either the name of the beast or the number of his name.

—REVELATION 13:16,17

The pages of history are filled with notorious rulers and leaders who have led nations to their demise. However, the Bible foretells another coming ruler who will lead the whole world down a path to destruction. The book of Revelation speaks about this individual, widely known as the Antichrist. Using every means at his disposal, including the technology of a cashless society, the Antichrist and his demands will bring the world into its greatest-ever moral and economic turmoil. Such chaos will make the stock market crash of 1929 look like a minor economic adjustment.

Revelation 13:16,17 is the biblical point of entry for discussion of the cashless society, a one-world government, global economics, and biblical prophecy. What we believe about biblical prophecy and its importance in our lives is vital to how we interpret the events which we read about daily in the newspapers, listen to on CNN, and discuss with friends and family. Biblical prophecy provides the lens through which to view the events and issues of our day. The headlines matter, economics matter, and prophecy matters. All three of these play a role in the present and the future.

What's Over the Horizon?

The Bible clearly predicts a future time of global turmoil, conflict, and deception. According to the biblical text, this will be a time in which a vast majority of the world's population will follow a leader whose evil desires and thirst for power will be unmatched in human history and will be contrary to the desires of God.

What is approaching us over the horizon, at some point in the future, is a time of despair and devastation. Will a cashless society be a part of this? We believe that either these events will transpire during the time of a cashless society and with the assistance of such technology, or that they will come in a post-cashless society in which technology has moved us beyond current cashless trends and speculation. How close are we to this time? Are there signs of its approach? The Bible provides answers to those who are willing to study, dig, and search the Scriptures in order to find them.

Does It Really Matter?

The God of the Bible claims to know the future. In fact, He confidently challenges His idolatrous rivals to predict future events. Guess what? They can't! And none of those psychics that make grand claims on late-night television know the future either. If they did, they would have a corner on the stock and commodity markets. These people are not experts on the future; instead, they have become experts on how to fool people who are open to superstition. Prophecy is the exclusive domain of God.

In the eighth century B.C., the Lord spoke through His prophet Isaiah:

> Remember the former things long past, for I am God, and there is no other; I am God, and there is no one like Me, declaring the end from the beginning and from ancient times things which have not been done, saying, "My purpose will be established, and I will accomplish all My good pleasure"; calling a bird of prey from the east, the man of My purpose from a far country. Truly I have spoken; truly I will bring it to pass. I have planned it, surely I will do it (Isaiah 46:9-11).

The Lord challenged His wayward people, who had fallen into idolatry, to compare Him with the impotent idols they were serving. Only the God of the Bible can prophesy the future with 100 percent accuracy. Again we read the Lord's bold declaration:

> I declared the former things long ago and they
> went forth from My mouth, and I proclaimed them.
> Suddenly I acted, and they came to pass. Because I
> know that you are obstinate, and your neck is an
> iron sinew, and your forehead bronze, therefore I
> declared them to you long ago, before they took
> place I proclaimed them to you, lest you should say,
> "My idol has done them, and my graven image and
> my molten image have commanded them." You
> have heard; look at all this. And you, will you not
> declare it? I proclaim to you new things from this
> time, even hidden things which you have not
> known (Isaiah 48:3-6).

Prophecy is unique to the Lord because He alone is eternal. Everything else and everyone is finite. Thus, the Israelites and their idols have a beginning and end. It could be said that man makes the idols, but God makes all things. Thus, God declares, "I am He, I am the first, I am also the last" (Isaiah 48:12). Because God is eternal and sovereign over creation, He alone knows the future. Only the Lord is capable of predicting history before it happens.

Over 300 specific biblical prophecies were fulfilled during the first coming of Christ almost 2000 years ago. Since every biblical prophecy thus far has been literally fulfilled, it follows that those remaining future prophecies should be viewed as history written in advance. About 20 percent of the Bible is prophecy that has yet to be fulfilled. In order to know God's outline of the future, we must not be afraid to study His Word and take it seriously.

Theologian Carl F.H. Henry says of contemporary society's aversion to prophetic truths:

The intellectual idolatries are many, all the more because they are cherished by those who have no patience with revealed religion, fixed truths, eternal commandments. The one "unthinkable" prospect of our technological society is (not the possibility of scientific destruction of modern civilization, for that prospect would congratulate the power potential of the scientific community, but rather) *divine doom!* The Second Coming of Christ, the End of all the ends, the gates of hell, the resurrection of the dead, the final judgment of mankind—these are all ruled out by the wisdom of the world. . . . So there arises a herd of humanity that anesthetizes the possibilities of spiritual life and knifes itself to spiritual death, a generation with mustard-seed consciences, a society that believes in pseudo-values and pseudo-truths.[1]

If we are to have any solid hope for the future, we must look to God's Word for guidance. In it are not only words of life, but words of *eternal* life.

The Prophetic Panorama

If you have ever worked jigsaw puzzles, you know that they can be tedious and time-consuming. When you start to work the puzzle, how do you go about it? If you are like us, you put all the pieces out on a table, place the box so that you can refer to its picture, and then start to put together the frame of the puzzle. Once the frame is completed, the hard work of putting the other individual pieces in place begins.

Studying prophecy is much like working a puzzle. Before you can make sense of the individual pieces, you first need to have the overall picture, a framework within which to set the pieces, and, second, you need to know that you have all the pieces. Only then can you be sure that it will all fit together. If you lose a piece or misjudge how it fits, the picture will be incomplete or wrong. How one interprets and applies prophecy is equally important. Dr. Charles C. Ryrie astutely observes of those who study and write on eschatology (the doctrine of last things):

> Prophecy seems to suffer at the hands of both its friends and foes. Friends sometimes overspeculate so that biblical passages are made to say more than they actually do; and foes overgeneralize so that the same passages are reduced to saying practically nothing.
>
> Bible prophecy is a major area of biblical revelation, and we must seek to understand what the Bible is saying for itself. Reading in the spectacular and the contemporary is no better than reading out the clear and specific.[2]

The "mark of the beast" in Revelation is one of the pieces of the prophetic puzzle. It's a small piece, but it is vital because without it the puzzle is incomplete. So, we must make sure we place it in its proper location. A correct understanding of Bible prophecy concerning the mark of the beast enables us to understand why we are racing toward globalism and a cashless society in our own time. Interpretations of "the mark," as well as perspectives on how the mark applies to contemporary society, must be neither overspeculated upon nor overgeneralized. We certainly want to look in-depth at this one piece of the puzzle, but not before seeing the entire prophetic picture and the pieces that comprise it.

Pieces of the Puzzle

The best way to grasp the big picture is to view each individual part and understand its relation to the whole. In the next several pages we will take a brief tour of the significant people and events of the last days, as recorded in the Scriptures.

Rapture

The rapture of the church is the next scheduled event on God's prophetic calendar.[3] The New Testament teaches that prior to a seven-year period of tribulation, all members of the church, the body of Christ (both living and dead), will be caught up in the air to meet Christ and then be taken to heaven. The teaching of the rapture is most clearly presented in 1 Thessalonians 4:13-18:

> But we do not want you to be uninformed, brethren, about those who are asleep, that you may not grieve, as do the rest who have no hope. For if we believe that Jesus died and rose again, even so God will bring with Him those who have fallen asleep in Jesus. For this we say to you by the word of the Lord, that we who are alive, and remain until the coming of the Lord, shall not precede those who have fallen asleep. For the Lord Himself will descend from heaven with a shout, with the voice of the archangel, and with the trumpet of God; and the dead in Christ shall rise first. Then we who are alive and remain shall be caught up together with them in the clouds to meet the Lord in the air, and thus we shall always be with the Lord. Therefore comfort one another with these words.

In this passage Paul informs his readers that living Christians at the time of the rapture will be reunited with those who have died in Christ before them. In verse 17 the English phrase "caught up" translates the Greek word *harpazó*, which means "to seize upon with force" or "to snatch up."

The rapture of the church is often paralleled to the "translations" or "raptures" of Enoch (Genesis 5:24) and Elijah (2 Kings 2:12). These raptures involved the removal of the person from earth to heaven. At the Lord's ascension, He too was taken "taken up" into heaven (Acts 1:9). The New Testament describes the coming rapture as an event in which believers, both dead and living, will rise in the air to meet the Lord (1 Thessalonians 4:16,17; 1 Corinthians 15:51,52).

We also see an illustration of the rapture concept in Acts 8:39, where Philip, upon completion of the baptism of the Ethiopian eunuch, was "caught up" and divinely transported from the desert to the coastal town of Azotus. Similarly, the church will, in a moment of time, be taken from earth to heaven.

The Tribulation

While we all experience trials and tribulation in our lives today, the Bible teaches that in the future there is coming a seven-year period that will be so severe it is commonly known as "the tribulation." Before the tribulation, Christ will return and rapture His church. At the end of the tribulation, Christ will return with the church to planet Earth. He will rescue Israel, judge unbelievers, and set up His 1000-year reign from Jerusalem, known as the Messiah's millennial kingdom. Daniel 9:24-27 first notes that the tribulation will be seven years in length, and this is confirmed throughout the book of Revelation. Scripture tells us it will begin as a result of an agreement between the people of Israel and the coming European ruler known as the Antichrist.

The Bible tells us more about the tribulation than about any other prophetic period. Throughout the Bible there are many direct and indirect references to the tribulation.[4] One of the earliest Old Testament passages to prophesy of this period in general is found in Deuteronomy 4:27-31. These verses foretell both the scattering of the Jews and their restoration to the Lord if they seek Him:

> And the LORD will scatter you among the peoples, and you shall be left few in number among the nations, where the LORD shall drive you. And there you will serve gods, the work of man's hands, wood and stone, which neither see nor hear nor eat nor smell. But from there you will seek the LORD your God, and you will find Him if you search for Him with all your heart and all your soul. When you are in distress and all these things have come upon you, in the latter days, you will return to the LORD your God and listen to His voice. For the LORD your God is a compassionate God; He will not fail you nor destroy you nor forget the covenant with your fathers which He swore to them.

Before Israel had set foot in their promised land, the Lord foretold their history in outline form in Deuteronomy. Part of their destiny includes a time of "distress" or "tribulation" (KJV) "in the latter days" right before Israel "will return to the LORD your God and listen to His voice." Later in Deuteronomy, Moses expands upon this time of tribulation. He notes that its purpose will include a time of retribution to the Gentiles for their ill-treatment of the Jews (Deuteronomy 30:7).

The purpose of the tribulation is for God to complete His dealings with the nation of Israel, which will lead to their recognition that Jesus of Nazareth is their Messiah. And it will be a time in which God will judge unbelieving Gentiles. Because of the purpose of the tribulation, the church will be removed at the rapture before the tribulation begins, since God's focus at that point in history will revolve around Israel. Therefore, it is highly significant that in 1948 Israel became a nation again, because God is preparing Israel and the world for this final period of history which will culminate in His return to reign on planet Earth for a thousand years. [5]

Major events of the tribulation include the following:

- The seal judgments (Revelation 6)
- The rise of Antichrist and the ten-nation confederacy (Daniel 2:42,44; 7:7,24; Revelation 12:3; 13:1; 17:12,16)
- The ministry of Elijah (Malachi 4:5,6)
- The revival through the 144,000 Jewish evangelists (Revelation 7)
- The trumpet judgments (Revelation 8–9)
- The ministry of the two witnesses (Revelation 11:3-6)
- The false church (Revelation 17:1-6)
- The little scroll (Revelation 10:9-11)
- The Antichrist killed (Revelation 13:3)
- Satan cast down to the earth from heaven (Revelation 12:7-9)
- The resurrection of the Antichrist (Revelation 13:3,4)

- Three kings killed and seven submit (Daniel 7:24; Revelation 17:12,13)
- Destruction of the false church (Revelation 17:16)
- The death and resurrection of the two witnesses (Revelation 11:7-13)
- Worship of the Antichrist (Revelation 13:3-8)
- The counterfeit ministry of the false prophet (Revelation 13:11-15)
- The mark of the beast—666 (Revelation 13:16-18)
- The seven-year covenant broken by the Antichrist (Daniel 9:27; Isaiah 28:18)
- The abomination of desolation (Daniel 9:27; Matthew 24:15,16; 2 Thessalonians 2:4)
- The bowl judgments (Revelation 16)
- The protection of the Jewish remnant (Micah 2:12; Matthew 24:16; Revelation 12:6,14)
- The conversion of Israel (Zechariah 12:10-14; Romans 11:25-27)
- The campaign of Armageddon (Isaiah 34; Joel 3; Zechariah 14:1-8; Revelation 16:14;19:17-21)
- The second coming of Jesus Christ (Daniel 2:44,45; Zechariah 14:3-5; Matthew 24:29-31; Revelation 19:11-21)

It is clear from the above outline of tribulation events that this will be a time clearly discernible in history.

The Second Coming of Christ

The second coming of Jesus Christ from heaven to earth is a hinge event ending the tribulation and preparing the way for the next major era of history, the 1000-year reign of Christ on earth, known as the millennium. Interestingly, narration of events surrounding the second coming are described in Revelation in relation to those who have received the mark of the beast:

> And the beast was seized, and with him the false prophet who performed the signs in his presence, by which he deceived those who had received the mark of the beast and those who worshiped his image; these two were thrown alive into the lake of fire which burns with brimstone. And the rest were killed with the sword which came from the mouth of Him who sat upon the horse, and all the birds were filled with their flesh (Revelation 19:20,21).

The last three-and-a-half years of the tribulation will be a time in which all unbelievers will receive the mark of the beast so that they may participate in the Antichrist's cashless economy. Thus, for the only time in history, an outward indication will identify those who reject Christ and His gospel of forgiveness of sins.

The Millennium

The tribulation as a time of judgment prepares the way for the 1000-year reign of Jesus Christ from Jerusalem. Many biblical passages describe this as a time in which Israel will be exalted, Jesus Christ will be present upon earth, and long life, peace, and righteousness will finally be an experienced reality. Yet there will still be sin and rejection of Jesus as the Christ. Revelation 20:1-10 provides an interesting picture of the millennium, which also views people in terms of the mark of the beast:

> And I saw an angel coming down from heaven, having the key of the abyss and a great chain in his hand. And he laid hold of the dragon, the serpent of old, who is the devil and Satan, and bound him for a thousand years, and threw him into the abyss, and shut it and sealed it over him, so that he should not deceive the nations any longer, until the thousand years were completed; after these things he must be released for a short time. And I saw thrones, and they sat upon them, and judgment was given to them. And I saw the souls of those who had been beheaded because of the testimony of Jesus and because of the word of God, and those who had not worshiped the beast or his image, and had not received the mark upon their forehead and upon their hand; and they came to life and reigned with Christ for a thousand years. The rest of the dead did not come to life until the thousand years were completed. This is the first resurrection. Blessed and holy is the one who has a part in the first resurrection; over these the second death has no power, but they will be priests of God and of Christ and will reign with Him for a thousand years. And when the thousand years are completed, Satan will be released from his prison, and will come out to deceive the nations which are in the four corners of the earth, Gog and Magog, to gather them together for the war; the number of them is like the sand of the seashore. And they came up on the broad plain of the earth and surrounded the camp of the saints and the beloved city, and fire came down from heaven and devoured them. And the devil who deceived them was thrown into the lake of fire and brimstone, where

the beast and the false prophet are also; and they will be tormented day and night forever and ever.

The millennium will be a time in which Satan and the Antichrist will be absent—thus, no mark of the beast or threat of satanic influence. The only source of evil during this time will spring from human nature. Then, at the end of the millennium a final judgment will take place in preparation for the new heavens and new earth of eternity.

Signs of the Times

As we mentioned, from our perspective today the next event on God's prophetic calendar will be the rapture of the church. In contrast to the second coming, the rapture is a "signless" event, in that the New Testament teaches it could happen at any moment. This explains why the church is to be in a state of perpetual readiness, because the rapture is imminent and will occur without warning. However, this does not mean that there are no "signs of the times" indicating that we could be near the end-time events.

In our overview of end-time prophecy you may have noticed the great detail with which the Bible speaks about the tribulation. Thus, a fairly detailed scenario or model can be developed from God's Word to give us a framework for comparing current world conditions with those of the future tribulation. Such a comparison indicates that our current world is being prepared for the tribulation.

Earlier we noted that the current world situation is like a stage being set for a future drama that will unfold. However, none of the current stage-setting provides a basis for specific date-setting. Date-setting is prohibited in the Bible (Matthew

24:36,42,44; 25:13; Mark 13:32-37; Acts 1:7; 1 Thessalonians 5:1,2). But we can confidently say that God is
preparing the world for the tribulation, and current events
indicate that the stage is being set.

The "super sign" of the end-times is the fact that Israel
has become a nation again. Many biblical passages dealing
with the tribulation picture a regathered nation of Israel
living in its own land but still persisting in unbelief. When
Israel became a nation again in 1948, it fulfilled the scenario
that the Bible predicted would precede the tribulation. Israel
makes all of the following signs significant, since nothing
would be significant if she were not on the scene.

Jerusalem is pictured during the tribulation as being
under Jewish control. This came to pass in 1967 when a par-
titioned Jerusalem came fully under Israeli sovereignty.

By the midpoint of the seven-year tribulation, the Bible
pictures a Jewish temple in Jerusalem that will be defiled by
the Antichrist (Daniel 9:27; Matthew 24:15; 2 Thessalonians
2:4; Revelation 11:1,2). This is not yet possible, but with
each passing year more Israelis are working toward the goal
of a rebuilt temple.[6]

The fact that Arab nations are the world leaders in oil
production that fuels Western economic development makes
their conflict with Israel of international importance. They
have been brought to such an important role in world affairs
because of the development of their oil reserves. Providing a
temporary solution to the current Middle East crisis will be
the Antichrist's entry onto the world scene as the tribulation
begins. Needless to say, the stage is clearly set for just such an
eventuality.

The Bible indicates that the Antichrist will arise as the leader of a revived Roman Empire, made up of a ten-nation confederation involving a unified Europe (Daniel 2:42,44; 7:7,24; Revelation 12:3; 13:1; 17:12,16, etc.), which will attempt to rule the world. Two world wars, the Cold War, NATO, and the United Nations have contributed in this century to the reunion of Europe and a push toward globalism. Today we see European unity already underway through the European Economic Community (EEC), which many see as a step toward a one-world government and the solution to global problems. The key to the unity of Europe is economic unity. Of course, the development of a cashless society helps to advance European economic development.

In 1948 ecumenicism and the world church movement formalized and continues to spread into the evangelical church and is preparing the way for the "superchurch" that will dominate the religious scene after the true church is raptured. The worldview shift in our day from Western rationalism to New Age mysticism, spiritism, the occult, and belief in demons continues to gain ascendency within secular culture and Christendom alike.

The Bible indicates that Russia and a coalition of Arab states will invade Israel during the last days (Ezekiel 38–39). Just such a scenario is possible as one examines current geopolitical developments. Israel had to be back in its land as a nation before such an alliance could attack Israel. Perhaps this is why in our day, for the first time in history, Russia has become a great military power. China continues to awaken and will play an increasing role in world events as God positions her for her military role outlined in Revelation 16.

Other key signs of the times could be noted,[7] but these are sufficient to make it clear that even though the God of the Bible is so often excluded from the daily lives of many, yet He, even through their rebellious actions, is preparing our globe for the coming tribulation. These contemporary developments, which relate to the rise of the revived Roman Empire out of which the Antichrist will arise and bring political, economic, and religious globalism, provide the context that gives biblical meaning to the current development of the coming cashless society.

The Cashless System of Revelation 13

The Bible does not specifically predict computers, the Internet, credit cards, or any of the other trimmings that facilitate the modern electronic banking system. However, the Bible does predict that during the tribulation an attempt will be made to control all economic activity. Why? The answer is ultimately a religious one. The economy will become an instrument through which every human being on planet Earth will be forced to manifest their choice between God and Satan, good and evil. Although many people in our day think that they can avoid God and His demands upon their lives by feigning neutrality, one's survival during the tribulation will be determined by a decision for or against God.

It is becoming increasingly apparent that today's developing cashless system will become the instrument through which the Antichrist will seek to control all who buy or sell, based upon whether they are a follower of Jesus Christ or a follower of the European ruler, and thus, Satan. It is obvious that any leader wanting to control the world's economy would avail themselves of the power that an electronic cashless system holds as a tool for implementing total control. Revelation 13:16,17 says,

> And he causes all, the small and the great, and the rich and the poor, and the free men and the slaves, to be given a mark on their right hand, or on their forehead, and he provides that no one should be able to buy or to sell, except the one who has the mark, either the name of the beast or the number of his name.

Speculation or Assumption?

Before moving on, we need to give a few words of caution. One of the greatest problems in interpreting Bible prophecy is the desire by overly zealous interpreters to read their own experiences into the passages. Dr. Ed Hindson states well the concern we should all maintain:

> When you study the *facts* of prophecy, be sure that you distinguish them from the *assumptions* you draw or the *speculations* you make. While we would all like to believe that our Lord will come in our lifetime, it is presumptuous to assume that we are the terminal generation. Surely He could come today, but then again He may not come for many years. That decision is up to God the Father.... The greatest danger of all in trying to interpret biblical prophecy is to assume that our speculations are true and preach them as facts.... The time has come when serious students of biblical prophecy must be

clear about what is fact, what is assumption, and
what is speculation. . . . Anything is possible but that
does not mean something is probable.[8]

Much of the contemporary discussion about prophecy
and technology combines excessive speculation and poor
interpretation. It is not our desire to add to such literature,
for sensationalism and speculation demean the Word of God
and its prophecies regarding the earth's last days.

We are not saying that those who are currently developing new economic technologies are evil or that their inten-
tions are evil. Most people in the industry probably have
little or no knowledge of biblical prophecy and its relationship to their research and products. But surely the coming
cashless society is one of the signs that prophecy is being fulfilled.

7

Visions of the Past and Future

DANIEL AND JOHN
SAW IT ALL

The apostle John and the prophet Daniel had much in common. Both men were fervent in their faith, and both recorded magnificent biblical prophecies which they received from the Lord. Though they lived 600 years apart, their messages are closely connected and intertwined. Daniel's prophecy does not have all of the prophetic intricacies recorded by John, nor does it reveal the depths of the glorious future of those who are God's own and worship Him. But Daniel does give the basic outline of Jewish and Gentile history, with an emphasis upon the yet-future seven-year tribulation. All the details of Bible prophecy are not contained in Daniel and Revelation alone, but the basic framework for prophecy is given in Daniel and expanded upon in Revelation. To understand how Bible students glean much of their insight into prophecy, we must therefore become familiar with these two most important biblical prophecy books. It is within this framework of "future history" that we will appreciate the role the coming cashless society will play in God's plan for mankind.

The Book of Daniel

The book of Daniel is about much more than lions, a fiery furnace, and Shadrach, Meshach, and Abednego. It is about the future. While the course of future events revolves around God's dealings with His elect nation of Israel, Daniel supplies an outline of Gentile history as well. Daniel provides the framework of prophetic history which is continued and completed in the New Testament book of Revelation.[1]

Back to the Future

The book of Daniel contains graphic prophetic visions that outline God's plan from the sixth century B.C., when Daniel lived and wrote, until the prophesied coming of Messiah's kingdom. The key prophetic chapters are Daniel 2, 7, 9, 11, and 12. Chapters 2, 7, and 9 provide chronological outlines for history from a Gentile and Jewish orientation. Key prophetic players and events are noted in Chapters 11 and 12. We must go back to Daniel in order to fully understand what God has revealed about the future.

In the days before sleeping pills, the Babylonian king, Nebuchadnezzar, had a distressing dream which, as it turns out, was an outline of Gentile history. Daniel, a Jewish captive, was summoned to the court of the troubled king, and through revelation from God he repeated the king's dream to him and interpreted it. This part of Daniel was originally written and recorded in Aramaic, a Gentile language, reinforcing the idea that Daniel 2 reports God's plan for history from a Gentile perspective.

Daniel 2:29-35 describes a large statue of a man whose body parts were made of different metals. The head was of pure gold, the chest area and arms were of silver, the hips and thighs were made of bronze, the legs were made of iron, and the feet were composed of part iron and baked clay. Next, Daniel saw a large stone that was cut out of a mountain without human hands, and it struck the feet of the statue, destroying the whole statue. Finally, the stone that destroyed the statue became a huge mountain and filled the whole earth.

Daniel explains the meaning of the dream in verses 36-45. He points out that history will be dominated by the rise to world power of a series of Gentile nations. These Gentile nations will rule the world until they are destroyed by a fifth and final kingdom: God's kingdom incorporating the nation of Israel. This period of Gentile domination and the four kingdoms, which started with the rise of Babylon in 586 B.C., is called "the times of the Gentiles" in the Bible. This means that world history will be dominated by a series of successive Gentile kingdoms, rather than by Israel, until God smashes the final form of the kingdoms of man in the last days.

Nebuchadnezzar and Babylon were the first Gentile kingdom, represented by the head of gold. The next kingdom to arise would be Medo-Persia, represented by the silver upper body. The third kingdom, made of bronze, would be

Greece, and the legs of iron represent Rome. The feet of iron and baked clay represent a yet-future revived Roman Empire coming from the fourth kingdom, and from which the Antichrist arises during the tribulation. The stone cut out of the mountain without hands refers to Christ, who at His second coming will smash the Antichrist and his kingdom and will set up His worldwide rule known as the millennial kingdom. This heavenly kingdom will be introduced suddenly and catastrophically, without being preceded by a long spiritual process which gradually conquers the earth. The heavenly kingdom does not join alongside of the current human government; instead, it replaces it with a righteous rule from heaven.

It has been rightly observed that each metal represents various characteristics of each kingdom. The ascribed worth of each metal declines in value as the dream progresses: gold (Babylon), silver (Medo-Persia), bronze (Greece), and iron (Rome), picturing the relative wealth of each kingdom. On the other hand, the sequence of metals indicates that each successive kingdom grew stronger than its predecessor. Daniel's prophecy was so accurate in its prediction of world events that critics have tried to say it was written after the fact, though there is no solid basis for such assumptions.

The king rewarded Daniel for his interpretation by giving him a promotion and increased responsibility. The dream is a vivid reminder that God, not men and women, is sovereign in world affairs. It is His breath that blows across the pages of history, raising and deposing empires and leaders. He is active in the large and small events of history and of our lives. From the dream we also learn that God has

Harmony of Daniel 2 and 7

	Chapter 2 Nebuchadnezzar's Dream of the Image		History	Chapter 7 Daniel's Vision of the Four Beasts	
	Prophecy		Fulfillment	Prophecy	
	Dream 2:31-35	Interpretation 2:36-45	World empires	Interpretation 7:15-28	Dream 7:1-14
1	2:32 Head (Gold)	2:38 Nebuchadnezzar	Babylonian 612-539 B.C.	7:17 King	7:4 Lion with wings of an eagle
2	2:32 Breast and arms (silver)	2:39 Inferior kingdom	Medo-Persian 539-331 B.C.	7:17 King	7:5 Bear raised up on one side
3	2:32 Belly and thighs (bronze)	2:39 Third kingdom	Grecian 331-63 B.C.	7:17 king	7:6 Leopard with four heads and four wings on its back
4	2:33 Legs (iron) feet (iron and clay)	2:40 Fourth Kingdom	Ancient Rome 63 B.C.–A.D. 476 / Revived Roman Empire (Rome)	7:23 Fourth kingdom / 7:24 Ten kings / 7:24 Different king	7:7,19 Fourth beast with iron teeth and claws of bronze / 7:7,8 Ten horns / 7:8 Little horn uttering great boasts
	2:35 Great mountain	2:44 Kingdom which will never be destroyed	Messianic kingdom	7:27 Everlasting kingdom	7:9 Thrones were set up

a plan for history and human events, and He is ordering history for that plan. He is setting the stage for a divine drama in which we are all participants.

Daniel 7: Daniel's Beastly Dream

A number of years after the events of Daniel 2, the prophet Daniel had a vision similar to that of Nebuchadnezzar. The events described are the same as those Nebuchadnezzar dreamed, but the perspective is different. Nebuchadnezzar's dream was recorded in the Aramaic language by the prophet, reflecting a Gentile perspective. In contrast, Daniel's dream in chapter 7 covers the same era, but from God's perspective, as reflected by the fact that it is recorded in Hebrew. That is why the kingdom of man is pictured as a succession of beasts.

Like Daniel 2, this vision repeats the theme of a succession of four Gentile empires that are overcome in the end by God's kingdom. Daniel 7 gives us additional information concerning the revived Roman Empire, which is yet future even to our own time. Daniel's vision begins with four beasts emerging from the sea. The depiction of the sea represents the masses of Gentile humanity (Isaiah 57:20; Revelation 17:15). God is telling us that these four beasts (i.e., empires) are the progeny of Gentile instability.

The identities of the four beasts are as follows:

- Babylon—a lion having the wings of an eagle (Daniel 7:4)
- Medo-Persia—a bear (verse 5)
- Greece—a leopard with four wings and four heads (verse 6)

• Rome—unspecified beast with iron teeth and bronze claws (verse 7).

In this vision, much more information is provided than in Daniel 2 regarding the revived Roman Empire of the tribulation. Clearly, the fourth kingdom is Rome, which crushed and dominated the kingdoms it conquered (Daniel 7:7). The ten horns represent a second phase of the Roman Empire, an empire which will reappear during the tribulation as the Antichrist's kingdom. The little horn is one of many synonyms describing the Antichrist, who will conquer the world through the revived Roman Empire. However, Daniel 7:11 foretells of his destruction by fire. The first three beasts and their kingdoms will merge with the fourth which will be destroyed, in its final form, by the cataclysmic coming of the Lord Jesus Christ in the fifth and final kingdom (Daniel 7:12).

Significantly, it is in this chapter of Daniel that we find an explanation of the activities of the one known as the Antichrist. This description is expanded upon in Revelation 13, as we will see later. The book of Daniel records these words:

> Thus he said: "The fourth beast will be a fourth kingdom on the earth, which will be different from all the other kingdoms, and it will devour the whole earth and tread it down and crush it. As for the ten horns, out of this kingdom ten kings will arise; and another will arise after them, and he will be different from the previous ones and will subdue three kings. And he will speak out against the Most High and wear down the saints of the Highest One, and he will intend to make alterations in times and in law;

and they will be given into his hand for a time, times, and half a time. But the court will sit for judgment, and his dominion will be taken away, annihilated and destroyed forever. Then the sovereignty, the dominion, and the greatness of all the kingdoms under the whole heaven will be given to the people of the saints of the Highest One; His kingdom will be an everlasting kingdom, and all the dominions will serve and obey Him" (Daniel 7:23-27).

John Walvoord observes of this passage:

The minute description given here of the end time, the fourth beast, and the ten horns followed by the eleventh horn that gained control of three has never been fulfilled in history. Some expositors have attempted to find ten kings of the past and the eleventh king who would arise to somehow fulfill this prophecy, but there is nothing corresponding to this in the history of the Roman Empire. The ten horns do not reign one after the other, but they reign simultaneously. Further, they were not the world empire, but they were the forerunner to the little horn which after subduing three of the ten horns will go on to become a world ruler (v. 23; Rev. 13:7).[2]

The career of the Antichrist can be summarized from these verses in five segments:

1. He will first conquer three of the ten rulers. This is how Antichrist will rise to power. He will come from one of the countries of the revived empire, according to Daniel's vision, and forcefully subdue three of the ten kings to become head of this Western federation of nations.

2. He will speak out against the true God of heaven (Daniel 7:25). The language indicates literally that he will attempt to raise himself to the level of God and make declarations from that supposed position. The apostle Paul predicts the same of this evil personage (2 Thessalonians 2:4).

3. He will persecute the saints (verse 25). Though believers of the present age will be removed from the earth at the coming of Christ for the church (John 14:1-3; 1 Thessalonians 4:13-18), many people will believe in Christ and be saved in the Tribulation which follows (see Revelation 7). For the believers, life will be difficult and even treacherous, particularly after Antichrist has come to power. He will harass, afflict, and persecute them without mercy and many will be martyred for their faith. The suffering of the saints will be particularly severe during the last half of the Tribulation, a period of three and one-half years.

4. He will attempt to change moral and natural laws of the universe, apparently without success (Daniel 7:25). An example of this may be seen in the attempt made by the leaders of the French Revolution to replace the seven-day week established by God with a ten-day week. Their efforts failed. On the other hand, Antichrist, energized by Satan, will be able to perform miracles which will cause many to accept his blasphemous claims and become his ardent followers (2 Thessalonians 2:8-11).

5. His career will come to a sudden and disastrous end (Daniel 7:26,27). The angel concludes his interpretive remarks by describing the fate of Antichrist, the "little horn" (see verse 11), and the establishment of a glorious kingdom on earth which the saints will inherit. This is

the kingdom of the Son of Man (verse 14), to be realized in the earthly, millennial reign of Jesus Christ. Thus Satan's counterfeit king and kingdom will be destroyed at Christ's coming to earth and the true King and kingdom will be established.[3]

It is this person who will use a future cashless system to control the world's economy as described in Revelation 13. However, the passage reminds us that history will not continue on its present course. Regardless of technological and scientific advances, the final act of history will be God's, in which he concludes the divine drama (Isaiah 64:1; Revelation 19:11).

Daniel 9: Daniel's Prayer and Prophecy

In 583 B.C., 67 years after Daniel had been taken captive by the Babylonians, he was studying the writings of a fellow prophet, Jeremiah, and realized that Israel's captivity was nearing its completion. Even though Daniel was just three years from the prophesied fulfillment of a biblical prophecy, this did not paralyze him or keep him from acting. He knew that the fulfillment of Israel's prophesied return to the land after 70 years of captivity was contingent on the fact that she confess her sins nationally. This drove Daniel to his knees to act on behalf of the nation. Daniel 9 records his prayer, which develops into a new revelation of God's prophetic time-line for Israel.

It appears from the flow of the context that Daniel believed his people would return from the Babylonian captivity and the promises of blessing made to Israel by God would soon come to pass. However, the Lord elongates

Daniel's chronological expectations. Not only would it be 70 more years, but Israel's history would include at least 70 weeks of years. Thus, God has not only given Daniel a prophetic outline of history (Daniel 2 and 7), but He now includes a chronology of Israel's future as well. Dr. Campbell writes of this passage:

1. The prophecy concerns the Jews and Jerusalem (v. 24). In contrast to the prophecies of chapters 2 and 7, which related to the Gentile nations, this prophecy portrays only God's program for Israel. The Church is not in view in any of these verses.

2. The scope of the prophecy covers not 70 years, as Daniel may have hoped, but 70 sevens of years. When Gabriel stated that 70 weeks were decreed concerning Jerusalem and the Jews he meant that that would be the length of time in which God would fulfill all of His purposes regarding the nation of Israel. The word for "week" is literally "sevens" or "hepstads." And it has been generally agreed since ancient times that the "weeks" or "sevens" are not weeks of days but weeks of years. Nothing else fits the context, for it is manifestly impossible to fit the events of 9:24-27 into 490 days or even weeks. The angel is thus saying to Daniel that 70 weeks of years, or a period of 490 years, is required to complete Israel's prophetic program.

3. This prophecy, it must be noted, concerns three deliverances. Daniel was greatly burdened about an early deliverance of the Jews from Babylon to return to Jerusalem. God was also interested in their deliverance from bondage to sin (at Christ's first advent) and in the final

deliverance of the Jews from oppression (at Christ's second coming).[4]

Daniel's Seventy Weeks

Daniel's "70 weeks," prophesied in Daniel 9:24-27, are the framework within which the tribulation or the seventieth week, occurs.[5]

> Seventy weeks have been decreed for your people and your holy city, to finish the transgression, to make an end of sin, to make atonement for iniquity, to bring in everlasting righteousness, to seal up vision and prophecy, and to anoint the most holy place. So you are to know and discern that from the issuing of a decree to restore and rebuild Jerusalem until Messiah the Prince there will be seven weeks and sixty-two weeks; it will be built again, with plaza and moat, even in times of distress. Then after the sixty-two weeks the Messiah will be cut off and have nothing, and the people of the prince who is to come will destroy the city and the sanctuary. And its end will come with a flood; even to the end there will be war; desolations are determined. And he will make a firm covenant with the many for one week, but in the middle of the week he will put a stop to sacrifice and grain offering; and on the wing of abominations will come one who makes desolate, even until a complete destruction, one that is decreed, is poured out on the one who makes desolate (Daniel 9:24-27).

The seven-year period of Daniel's seventieth week provides the time span with which a whole host of descriptives are associated. These descriptive terms include the following: *tribulation, great tribulation, day of the Lord, day of wrath, day of distress, day of trouble, time of Jacob's trouble, day of darkness and gloom, wrath of the Lamb*, etc. A graphic presentation of the 70 weeks assists greatly in understanding this intricate prophecy:

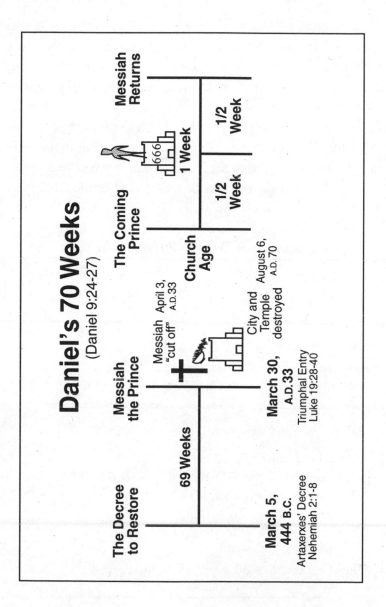

The chart of Daniel's 70 weeks presents a premillennial pretribulational perspective. That is, it shows the rapture occurring before the tribulation and the second coming of Christ before the millennium. Although not all evangelicals hold to a pretribulational rapture (some favoring instead a midtribulational or posttribulational view), there is agreement that the Antichrist will arise during the tribulation. He may be known, recognized, or even in power before the rapture, but he will be revealed or manifested as the Antichrist only during the tribulation (2 Thessalonians 2:6,8).

Explanation of Daniel's 70 Weeks of Years

69 x 7 x 360 = 173,880 days
March 5, 444 B.C. + 173,880 = March 30, A.D. 33

Verification

444 B.C. to A.D. 33 = 476 years
476 years x 365.242189 days = 173,855 days
+ days between March 5 and March 30 = 25 days
Total = 173,880 days

Rationale for 360-Day Years

1/2 week—Daniel 9:27
Time, times, 1/2 time—Daniel 7:25, 12:7; Revelation 12:14
1260 days—Revelation 12:6; 11:3
42 months—Revelation 11:2; 13:5
Thus: 42 months = 1260 days = time, times,
    1/2 time + 1/2 week
Therefore: month = 30 days; year = 360 days[6]

Cashless Calculations

How does the cashless society fit into Daniel's prophetic calculations? It is during this time of the tribulation, specifically from the midpoint to the end of the seven years, that a cashless society will most probably be enacted to control commerce and people. This corresponds with John's vision, 600 years later, as recorded in Revelation 13:17: "He provides that no one should be able to buy or to sell, except the one who has the mark."

But what about the 70th week of this prophecy? If we follow the principle of literal interpretation, we must conclude that the final week of years is still future, because the phenomena described in verse 27 have simply not yet occurred. Furthermore, Jesus said (Matt. 24:15) that when the abomination of desolation appeared in the temple, it would mean the onset of the Great Tribulation, which is to be immediately followed by the second advent of Christ. Likewise, the person described in Daniel 9:27 is clearly the same as the wicked individual of Daniel 7:25 and Revelation 12 and 13, and that person is judged at Christ's second coming (Rev. 19:20). The day is coming, therefore, when God's prophetic program for Israel will be resumed. This will be signaled by the signing of a seven-year covenant with the restored Jewish nation by a certain person (Dan. 9:27). This person can be identified as a prince of the people who destroyed the city and the sanctuary, that is, a Roman prince. He is none other than Antichrist, the "little horn" of Daniel 7, the eventual head of the revived Roman empire of the Tribulation period.[7]

Daniel's prophecy provides us with a clear foundation and framework regarding future events which John expands upon in Revelation. A key element of this time will be the economic control exerted by the Antichrist. A clear presentation of future tribulation events gives us a clear perspective with which to see the significance of the emergence of a cashless society today. Daniel's prophecy is rich in insight: The Antichrist will have great economic control for a period of time, but he will prove to be spiritually bankrupt. The book of Revelation provides the most detailed material about the Antichrist and his coming cashless agenda.

The Book of Revelation

Even though the Bible was written by dozens of human authors over a thousand years, its single Divine author ensures internal consistency rarely found in a normal human work. Thus, it is not surprising that God would provide an expansion of the book of Daniel in the New Testament. Revelation expands upon the book of Daniel and includes material relating to the church; something not found in Daniel.

A Prophetic Play in Three Acts

John's vision was recorded late in the first century, while he was a political and religious exile on the island of Patmos. As a young man John had been an eyewitness of the life and ministry of the Lord Jesus Christ. So close was he to the Lord that in the Gospel of John, when telling of the crucifixion, he refers to himself as "the disciple whom He loved" (John 19:26). It is this friend and disciple to whom a dramatic

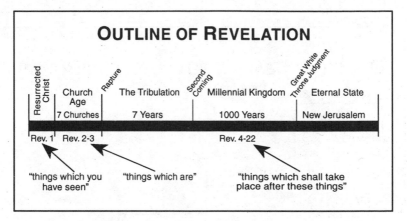

revelation of future events is given. How fitting it was that one who was so close to the Lord while He walked the earth would be the recipient of such a magnificent message.

In John's revelation, history is divided into three epochs. According to Revelation 1:19, John was instructed to "Write therefore *the things which you have seen, and the things which are, and the things which shall take place after these things*" (emphasis added). Thus, the book of Revelation divides into the following sections:

1. The things which you have seen (Revelation 1)
2. The things which are (Revelation 2,3)
3. The things which shall take place after these things (Revelation 4–22)

As you can see from the chart on the following page, Revelation 4 and following is the most extensive and detailed description of tribulation events recorded in God's Word. We have seen that the tribulation is first mentioned in Deuteronomy 4:27-31, referred to throughout the prophets, and revealed as a seven-year period in Daniel 9:24-27. In John's

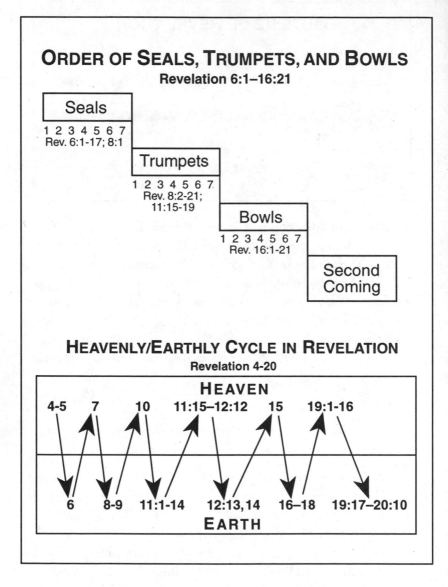

ORDER OF SEALS, TRUMPETS, AND BOWLS
Revelation 6:1–16:21

Seals

1 2 3 4 5 6 7
Rev. 6:1-17; 8:1

Trumpets

1 2 3 4 5 6 7
Rev. 8:2-21;
11:15-19

Bowls

1 2 3 4 5 6 7
Rev. 16:1-21

Second Coming

HEAVENLY/EARTHLY CYCLE IN REVELATION
Revelation 4-20

HEAVEN

4-5   7   10   11:15–12:12   15   19:1-16

6   8-9   11:1-14   12:13,14   16–18   19:17–20:10

EARTH

writings about the tribulation, we learn that the Antichrist will control the world's economy, almost certainly through a cashless society.

Tracking the Tribulation

Revelation 4-19 progresses in a chronological fashion. But there are periodic pauses in the sequence to introduce key figures and to alternate between a heavenly and an earthly perspective. Graphically portrayed, these chapters look like this:

A Heavenly Perspective (Chapters 4–5)

Throughout Revelation there is a cycling between the heavenly perspective (God's perspective) and the earthly perspective (human perspective). It is important to note that the section on the tribulation (Revelation 4–19) begins with the heavenly perspective. As we move from Revelation 2 and 3 (representative of the present church age), to Revelation 4–19 (the tribulation section), John is summoned by a heavenly voice to "come up here, and I will show you what must take place after these things" (Revelation 4:1). Thus John, as a representative of the church, is found in heaven. Dr. Walvoord says of chapters 4,5:

> One of the important conclusions in prophecy is the concept that the church composed of the saved of the present age will be in heaven while the great events of the Tribulation and of the end time take place. This is exactly what is described in Revelation 4-5. The church in heaven is in contrast to the great time of trouble which will take place on the earth prior to the second coming of Christ. Accordingly,

though the specific prophecies of 4-5 are not the main burden of these two chapters, what is being described is a vision of heaven when the saints and angels and the sovereign God on His throne form an intelligent background for other events that shall take place both in heaven and on earth.[8]

The Lord's Prayer contains the request, "Thy kingdom come, Thy will be done, on earth as it is in heaven." Revelation 4,5 is the beginning of a seven-year period that definitely answers this request.

Chapter 4 introduces us to the heavenly drama of the need for someone who is worthy to execute God's mandate. Chapter 5 shows us that Jesus Christ is the only One worthy to take the title deed of earth and execute its mandate.

The Battle Begins: The Seal Judgments (Chapter 6)

Many of the judgments of Revelation revolve around three series of judgments: seals, trumpets, and bowls. The descriptions of the three series of judgments appear to show that the seals represent the beginning of judgment, the trumpets represent the continuation of judgment, and the bowls represent the climax of God's judgment.

Chapter 6 tells of the six seal judgments, the first four of which are depicted as horses and riders. The first rider comes on a white horse and represents the Antichrist's intent to conquer the world (6:2). The second rider approaches on a red horse and is symbolic of war (6:3,4). The third seal and rider is a black horse representing famine (6:5,6). The final horse and rider is ashen, portraying death (6:7,8). The fifth seal is martyrdom and is related to events of the tribulation

Tribulation Events As Described in Revelation

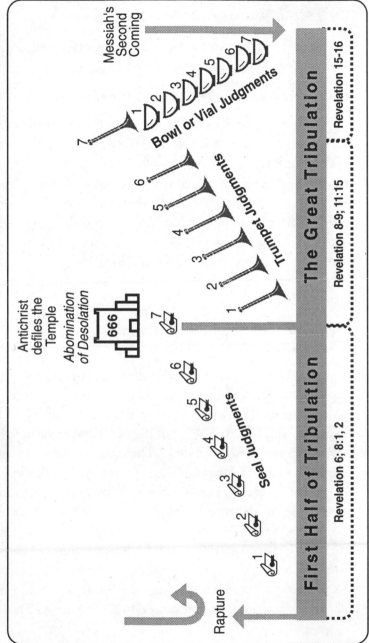

(6:9-11). The sixth and final seal involves catastrophic judgment through natural disasters (6:12-17).

The Redeemed of the Tribulation (Chapter 7)

Chapter 7 returns us to the heavenly perspective in which there is a temporary suspension of the judgments. Verses 2-8 speak of the sealing of the 144,000 Jewish evangelists and verses 9-17 describe the salvation of Gentiles of many nationalities. The fact that these two saved multitudes (Jews and Gentiles) are present on earth during the tribulation indicates that even though there will be great calamity, there will also be many who come to the cross of Christ for salvation.

From here the perspective moves back to earth in the next two chapters.

The Battle Continues: The Trumpet Judgment (Chapters 8–9)

The second series of judgments is identified as trumpet judgments, perhaps because they all are implemented through angels. The first trumpet judgment involves hail and fire mixed with blood. A third of the earth and trees and all of the green grass is destroyed (8:7). The second trumpet involves a fiery mountain thrown into the sea resulting in a third of the sea, becoming blood, a third of sea life dying, and a third of the sea's ships destroyed (8:8,9). The third trumpet is a burning star named Wormwood cast into the sea so that one-third of the rivers and the earth's fresh water supplies become bitter and many people die (8:10,11). In the fourth, one-third of the heavens are smitten so that one-third of the heavenly light is diminished, affecting both day and night (8:12).

The fifth judgment is preceded by a warning, and then a plague of locusts attacks unbelievers, tormenting them for five months (8:13–9:11). The sixth and final trumpet judgment involves a 200-million-man army destroying one-third of humanity (9:13-21).

Big Surprise: The Small Scroll (Chapter 10)

This chapter returns to the heavenly perspective; it is a time of preparation in which there is a long pause in John's presentation of the campaign of heaven against earth. A small opened scroll is held by an angel; it contains seven thunders; and is apparently a revelation about the mystery of God that will finally be revealed in Christ's second coming. This announcement is viewed as bittersweet. Initially it is sweet to know of the Lord's glorious return, but the judgments that accompany His return will be a bitter experience for many people.

A Lineup of Many Players (Chapters 11–15)

You can't know the players without a scorecard. In the middle of John's vision, many personalities are introduced, along with descriptions of their roles in the tribulation. The introduction of these key players prepares the reader of Revelation for the all-important second half of the tribulation, known as "the great tribulation."

We know from Daniel 9:27 and Matthew 24:15 that the great tribulation begins with "the abomination of desolation." Second Thessalonians 2:3,4 informs us that this event occurs when the "man of lawlessness," the Antichrist, "takes his seat in the temple of God, displaying himself as being God." Revelation 13:15 adds to the picture: "And there was given to him to give breath to the image of the beast, that the image of the beast might even speak and cause as many as do not worship the image of the beast to be killed." Such an act of evil arrogance demands a response from heaven. Thus, the judgments of God in the second half of the tribulation increase in intensity leading up to the battle of Armageddon and the second coming of Christ. But first, who are the players?

Revelation 11 opens with a description of the tribulation temple, which has been rebuilt by the midpoint of the tribulation (verses 1,2). It is within this context that we are introduced to the ministry of the two witnesses in Jerusalem. Paul Benware says:

> God will raise up two special individuals in the Tribulation who will bear testimony for Him. They will be given the ability to work powerful miracles (vv. 5-6), which will validate their ministry to the people of Israel as being from God. Their ministry is centered in the city of Jerusalem, which is identified in the text by the phrase "where also their Lord was crucified" (v. 8). Though the content of their message is not given, the fact that they are clothed in sackcloth (v. 3) suggests that their emphasis will be similar to that of John the Baptist, who was also a wearer of sackcloth (Matt. 3:4). . . . Revelation 11:7 states that when they have completed their ministry they will be put to death by the Antichrist. This terrible act will cause the unbelieving world to rejoice and celebrate. But, much to their amazement, the two witnesses will be raised from the dead and taken to heaven. Their resurrection, like that of the Lord Jesus, will give clear testimony to the fact that the Father approved their ministry.[9]

Revelation 12 introduces us to several new personalities who are active during the second half of the tribulation. First we see "a woman clothed with the sun" (verse 1), which represents the nation of Israel. This woman gives birth to "a male child" (verse 5), which represents the Lord Jesus Christ and describes His career. The extreme anti-Semitism of the tribulation is pictured by the dragon (Satan) who persecutes the woman (Israel) who "fled into the wilderness where she had a place prepared by God, so that there she might be nourished for one thousand two hundred and sixty days" (verse 6). Many scholars believe that this refers to Petra in modern-day Jordan. Satan will attack Israel after he is expelled from heaven by Michael and his angels at the midpoint of the tribulation. As a result, he will vent his fury upon God's people—Israel.

The beast (the Antichrist) bounds onto the stage as we approach Revelation 13. As was seen in Daniel 7:3, the beast is presented as "coming up out of the sea" (verse 1). The collective evil of previous Gentile empires is pictured as concentrated in the beast of Revelation 13:2. The beast imitates the one whom he wishes to usurp—Jesus Christ. Thus, the beast is fatally wounded and comes back to life feigning a counterfeit resurrection:

> And I saw one of his heads as if it had been slain, and his fatal wound was healed. And the whole earth was amazed and followed after the beast; and they worshiped the dragon, because he gave his authority to the beast; and they worshiped the beast, saying, "Who is like the beast, and who is able to wage war with him?" (Revelation 13:3,4).

This event is the springboard for his demand of worldwide worship during the last half of the tribulation and will be the time when he employs the cashless system in an effort to control the economy.

Some have nicknamed the beast of Revelation 13 "the Mouth," because Scripture presents him as one who frequently is "speaking arrogant words and blasphemies" (verse 5). He persecutes to the death those who do not submit to his will, but he is worshiped by non-Christians (verses 7,8).

Revelation 12 and 13 have introduced us to the first two members of the satanic trinity. Satan (the dragon) corresponds to God the Father (chapter 12); the beast (the Antichrist) corresponds to the Son (the first half of chapter 13); and now we learn of the false prophet, who corresponds to the Holy Spirit (the rest of chapter 13).

The false prophet uses religion to support the political career of the Antichrist. J. Dwight Pentecost summarizes the person and activities of the false prophet:

1. He is a Jew arising out of the earth, e.g., Palestine (13:11).

2. He is religiously influential (13:11).

3. He is motivated by Satan (13:11).

4. He has a delegated authority (13:12).

5. He promotes worship of the first beast (13:12).

6. He performs signs and miracles (13:13,14).

7. He deceives the unbelieving world (13:14).

8. He promotes idolatrous worship (13:14,15).

9. He has the power of death over people who do not worship the beast (13:15).

10. He has great economic power (13:16,17).

11. He will establish the mark of the beast (13:17).[10]

Revelation 14 reintroduces us to the Lamb and to the 144,000 witnesses. They are Jewish evangelists protected by God in preparation of those specially sealed for the last half of the tribulation, in which the Antichrist will demand proof of allegiance by receiving his number, 666. Jesus Christ's depiction as the Lamb focuses upon His redemptive work for sinners—the message of the 144,000.

A series of three angels are sent to earth from heaven with messages from God (Revelation 14:6-12). The first angel preaches the gospel and God's impending judgment to those on the earth. The second angel announces, "Fallen, fallen is Babylon the great, she who has made all the nations drink of the wine of the passion of her immorality" (verse 8). The last angel announces the following:

> If anyone worships the beast and his image, and receives a mark on his forehead or upon his hand, he also will drink of the wine of the wrath of God, which is mixed in full strength in the cup of His anger; and he will be tormented with fire and brimstone in the presence of the holy angels and in the presence of the Lamb. And the smoke of their torment goes up forever and ever; and they have no rest day and night, those who worship the beast and his image, and whoever receives the mark of his name. (Revelation 14:9-11).

The final verses of Revelation 14 describe the Lord sending out angels in judgment, as a farmer sends out workmen to the fields to harvest ripe grain. Dr. Walvoord explains the significance:

> Revelation 14 gathers in one perspective the major elements of the end-time judgments, including the 144,000 as a token of God's delivering power, the prediction of the fall of Babylon which is a major factor of the period of the second coming of Christ, the doom of the armies that oppose Christ at His second coming, the judgment on the world ruler, the beast and his assistant, the false prophet, the blessedness of those who die in the period of the Great Tribulation because of their immediate release to heaven, and, finally, the accuracy and justice of God's judgment on religious apostasy, and blasphemy against God which describes the end-time period.[11]

Revelation 14 could be described as a massive "warning campaign" implemented by God before He launches His final volley of judgment.

Revelation 15 introduces us to the seven angels who are poised in heaven, ready to carry out the final series of plagues known as the bowl judgments.

The Battle Concludes: The Bowl Judgments (Chapter 16)

Unlike the previous seal and trumpet judgments, the seven plagues of the bowls are poured out quite rapidly and without interruption. The bowl judgments proceed as follows:

1. A plague of "loathsome and malignant sores" upon those having the mark of the beast (verse 2).

2. The sea is turned to blood, killing every living thing in it (verse 3).

3. Every river and spring of water on the earth is turned to blood (verse 4).

4. The sun scorches non-Christians with intense heat (verses 8,9).

5. The beast and his kingdom are inflicted with such pain that "they gnawed their tongues because of pain" (verses 10,11).

6. The Euphrates River is dried up to facilitate the passage of armies into the land of Israel for the battle of Armageddon (verse 12).

7. A judgment of chaos in nature, including earthquakes and huge hailstones about 100 pounds each (verses 17-21).

Bye, Bye, Babylon (Chapters 17,18)

Why Babylon? Why does the book of Revelation devote two major chapters to a description and judgment of Babylon? Babylon expert Charles Dyer notes,

> From Genesis to Revelation, Babylon occupies a prominent place in the Bible. Babylon epitomizes humanity's pride and rebellion against God. The name comes from the description of the tower around which the city was first built—bab (gate), el (god). Babel was humanity's self-appointed gateway to God, the place where they hoped to reach God by their efforts apart from His intended plan.
>
> Babylon retained its essential nature throughout the Bible. The height of Babylon's opposition to God came

when the army of Babylon destroyed Jerusalem and dismantled God's kingdom on earth. They deposed the king from the line of David and dragged him off in chains. They burned the temple of Solomon and carried off the people of Judah. Daniel described Babylon as the "head of gold" in the "times of the Gentiles"—that time when Gentile powers would rule over God's people.

But the God who predicted the triumph of Babylon also promised its ultimate destruction.[12]

God is going to judge Babylon because of her supreme legacy as the opponent of God's people and program. The "times of the Gentiles" begins with Babylon and ends with her judgment. Thus, Revelation 17,18 focuses upon Babylon as the repository of satanic and human opposition to God and His program.

It's Not Over Till...

The tribulation finally comes to an end in Revelation 19. Christ's return to earth is preceded by heavenly activity. His bride, the church, has been in heaven throughout the tribulation and has made herself ready to return with Him. Revelation 19:11-16 describes Christ's demeanor as He readies for His return. At the second coming, Christ's first act is the destruction of His enemies:

> And I saw the beast and the kings of the earth and their armies, assembled to make war against Him who sat upon the horse, and against His army. And the beast was seized, and with him the false prophet who performed the signs in his presence, by which he deceived those who had received the mark

of the beast and those who worshiped his image; these two were thrown alive into the lake of fire which burns with brimstone. And the rest were killed with the sword which came from the mouth of Him who sat upon the horse, and all the birds were filled with their flesh (Revelation 19:19-21).

With these verses, Antichrist's reign of terror—including his religious, political, and economical program, is forever destroyed. His evil use of the cashless system will be brought to an end. Because God is righteous, He will not allow the progress of evil to continue indefinitely, but will one day judge it.

In Revelation 20 the brilliance of the millennial rule of Christ provides a stark contrast to the darkness of the tribulation. This will also mean the end of the evil of the cashless society's technology and resources. If they are to be employed after that, they will be used justly.

8

Biometrics
and the Beast
THE COMING ANTICHRIST

*And he cried out with a mighty voice, saying,
"Fallen, fallen is Babylon the great! And she has
become a dwelling place of demons and a prison
of every unclean spirit, and a prison of every
unclean and hateful bird. For all the nations
have drunk of the wine of the passion of her
immorality, and the kings of the earth have
committed acts of immorality with her, and the
merchants of the earth have become rich by the
wealth of her sensuality"* (Revelation 18:2,3).

He who has the gold, makes the rules," is a popular
slogan. At no time in all of history will its truth be
more evident than during the second half of the tribulation.

Babylon: A Biblical Wall Street

Throughout the Bible, Babylon is portrayed as the major
commercial entity with enormous prophetic significance.

Nebuchadnezzar and his empire, Babylon, are depicted as the head of gold on the figure in Daniel 2, implying great wealth. From Genesis to Revelation, the Bible associates Babylon with economic prosperity. Babylon has vast wealth. It is "the beauty of kingdoms" (Isaiah 13:19), "the golden city" (Isaiah 14:4), "a golden cup" from which "all the nations have drunk" (Jeremiah 51:7). It is "abundant in treasures" (Jeremiah 51:13).[1] Even extrabiblical tradition credits the second millennium B.C. ruler Hammurabi as the father of fractional reserve banking and inflation. Thus, it is not surprising to find a biblical association in Revelation 18 between Babylon, the Antichrist, and commerce.

Revelation 17 and 18 articulate a relationship seen across the pages of Scripture. Religion, politics, and economics are consistently intertwined and associated with Babylon, a synonym for the kingdom of man. Economics and politics have always been employed by those who would usurp devotion reserved only for God. Such a mixture will reach its zenith under Antichrist's tyranny during the tribulation. The focus of his coercive economic policies will revolve around the well-known mark of the beast—666.

The Tribulation Trademark: 666!

The core issue of the tribulation period is, "Who has the right to rule—God or Satan?" God will demonstrate unequivocally that He has the right to rule. For the only time in history, people will have a deadline for declaring their allegiance to the gospel. Throughout the past 2000 years, people have been at different stages in deciding for or against acceptance of the gospel. People accept or reject this message at various points in their lives: some in childhood, some as young adults, some at middle age or as seniors. On this occasion the process will be accelerated or forced because of the mark of the beast, so that all humanity will be consciously divided into two segments. The polarizing issue is the mark of the beast.

> And I saw another beast coming up out of the earth; and he had two horns like a lamb, and he spoke as a dragon. And he exercises all the authority of the first beast in his presence. And he makes the earth and those who dwell in it to worship the first beast, whose fatal wound was healed. And he performs great signs, so that he even makes fires come down out of heaven to the earth in the presence of men.
>
> And he deceives those who dwell on the earth because of the signs which it was given him to perform in the presence of the beast, telling those who dwell on the earth to make an image to the beast who had the wound of the sword and has come to life. And there was given to him to give breath to the image of the beast, that the image of the beast might even speak and cause as many as do not worship the image of the beast to be killed.
>
> And he causes all, the small and the great, and the rich and the poor, and the free men and the slaves, to be given a mark on their right hand, or on their forehead, and he provides that no one should be able to buy or to sell, except the one who has the mark, either the name of the beast or the number of his name.
>
> Here is wisdom. Let him who has understanding calculate the number of the beast, for the number is that of a man; and his number is six hundred and sixty-six (Revelation 13:11-18).

The mark of the beast has been the focal point of more rhetoric, ridicule, argumentation, and speculation than possibly any other single item in the Bible. The Bible teaches that it will be the false prophet, who is the spokesman for false religion, who will head up the campaign for the mark of the beast (Revelation 13:11-18). Revelation 13:15 makes it clear that the key issue is "worship [of] the image of the beast." The mark of the beast is simply a vehicle to force people to choose their allegiance—to the Antichrist or to Jesus Christ. All people will be polarized into two camps. It will be impossible to take a position of neutrality or indecision on this matter. Scripture is clear that those who do not receive the mark will be killed.

All classes of humanity will be forced to take sides: "the small and the great, and the rich and the poor, and the free men and the slaves" (Revelation 13:16). Dr. Robert Thomas notes that this language "extends to all people of every civic rank . . . all classes ranked according to wealth . . . covers every cultural category. . . . The three expressions are a formula for universality."[2]

Scripture is specific: The false prophet will require a "mark" of loyalty and devotion to the beast, and it will be "on their right hand," not the left, "or on their forehead" (Revelation 13:16).

Throughout the Bible, the word "mark" is employed. For example, it is used many times in Leviticus as a reference to a mark that renders the subject ceremonially unclean, usually related to leprosy. Interestingly, Ezekiel 9:4 uses "mark" similarly to the way it is used in Revelation: "And the LORD said to him, 'Go through the midst of the city, even through the midst of Jerusalem, and put *a mark on the foreheads* of the men who sigh and groan over all the abominations which are being committed in its midst.'" Here the mark was one of preservation, similar to the way that blood on the doorposts spared those in the passover from the death angel. In Ezekiel, the mark is placed on the forehead, which anticipates Revelation's use of the term. All seven instances of the Greek word for "mark" or "sign," *charagma*, in the Greek New Testament appear in Revelation, and all refer to "the mark of the beast" (Revelation 13:16,17; 14:9,11; 16:2; 19:20; 20:4). Dr. Thomas explains how the word was used in ancient times:

> The mark must be some sort of branding similar to that given soldiers, slaves, and temple devotees in John's day. In Asia Minor, devotees of pagan religions delighted in the display of such a tattoo as an emblem of ownership by a certain god. In Egypt, Ptolemy Philopator I branded Jews, who submitted to registration, with an ivy leaf in recognition of their Dionysian worship (cf., 3 Macc. 2:29). This meaning resembles the long-time practice of carrying signs to advertise religious loyalties (cf., Isa. 44:5) and follows the habit of branding slaves with the name or special mark of their owners (cf., Gal. 6:17). *Charagma* ("Mark") was a term for the images or names of emperors on Roman coins, so it fittingly could apply to the beast's emblem put on people.[3]

Some wonder why an exclusive term—"mark"—is used to designate Antichrist's mark. Antichrist's mark appears to be a parody of the plan of God, especially God's "sealing" of the 144,000 witnesses of Revelation 7. God's seal of His witnesses most likely is invisible and for the purpose of protection from the Antichrist. On the other hand, Antichrist offers protection from the wrath of God—a promise he cannot deliver—and his mark is visible and external. Since those receiving the mark of the beast take it willingly, it must be a point of pride to have Satan, in essence, as one's owner. Dr. Thomas says that the term "mark" denotes "loyalty, owner-ship, and protection," just as the seal given the slaves of God. The verb (*charassô*, "I engrave") is the source of *charagma* (cf. Acts 17:29). It will be visible and the point of recognition for all in subjection to the beast."[4]

The Treacherous Ticket

In addition to serving as a visible indicator of devotion to the Antichrist, the mark will be one's required ticket for com-mercial transactions during the last half of the tribulation. Revelation 13:17 says, "And he provides that no one should be able to buy or to sell, except the one who has the mark, either the name of the beast or the number of his name." This has been the dream of every tyrant down through his-tory—to so totally control his subject that he alone decides who can buy or sell. Historian Sir William Ramsay notes that, in the days when the book of Revelation was given to the apostle John, Roman emperor Domitian "carried the theory of Imperial Divinity and the encouragement of 'dela-tion' to the most extravagant point . . . that in one way or another every Asian must stamp himself overtly and visibly as loyal, or be forthwith disqualified from participation in ordinary social life and trading."[5] It will be left to the yet future leader of the revived Roman Empire to perfect such a practice with the aid of the coming cashless society and modern computer technology.

Many have tried down through history to mark certain groups of people for death. Yet there have always been ways for a certain number to hide or escape oppression. As technology becomes more advanced, it seems that greater potential will exist to close up virtually every means of escape. Just such a picture is supported by the Greek word *dunétai*, "provides," in Revelation 13:17, which is used to convey an idea of what "can" or "cannot" be done. The Antichrist will not allow anyone to buy or sell without the mark, and the coming cashless society will be the means that he will use to enact his policy. Control of the economy at the individual level through the mark fits perfectly with the biblical picture of Antichrist's control of global commerce as outlined in Revelation 17 and 18.

The second half of verse 17 describes the mark as "either the name of the beast or the number of his name." Precisely, this means that the "number of the beast's name is one and the same with the name. . . . The equivalence means that as a name, it is written in letters, but as a number, the name's equivalent is in numbers."[6] The Antichrist's name will be expressed numerically as "666."

Calculating the Number

Here is wisdom. Let him who has understanding calculate the number of the beast, for the number is that of a man; and his number is six hundred and sixty-six (Revelation 13:18).

The apostle John at this point in the prophecy shifts from one who is recording what he sees to one who now advises his readers in how to interpret what has been reported.

A reading of Revelation reveals that the wicked will not understand because of their moral rejection of Jesus Christ as Lord and Savior. In contrast, wisdom and understanding will be given to people during the tribulation to know who the Antichrist is, so that they will not take his mark. The Bible makes it abundantly clear that anyone taking the mark of the beast cannot be saved (Revelation 14:9,11; 16:2; 19:20; 20:4). Those who take the mark will spend eternity in the lake of fire, commonly known as hell. The fact that John provides wisdom and understanding to believers at this crucial point, relating to a matter of eternal importance, shows that God will provide the knowledge His people need to follow Him faithfully.

What does this wisdom and understanding allow the believer to do? The passage says he will be able to "calculate." Calculate what? He will be able to calculate the number of the beast.

The primary purpose for warning believers about the mark is to let them know that when it is in the form of numbers the "name" of the beast will be 666. Instead of predicting his name, John has received revelation that a shortened version of the name of the beast will be in the form of the number 666. Thus, believers who are going through the sequence of events of the tribulation, when offered the number 666 for their forehead or right hand, are to reject it, even if it means death. This also means that anything prior to this future time period is not the mark of the beast that is to be avoided.

Thus, Christians in our own day do not need to act superstitiously about the number. If our address, phone number, or zip code includes this number, we do not need to be afraid that some satanic or mystical power will influence us. On the other hand, we do recognize that many occultists and satanists are attracted to the number because of its relation to a future evil time. We have seen the number used by occultists, and in the last few years a number of rock bands have used the number. However, the number itself does not contain mystical powers. To believe that it does would mean that a believer has fallen prey to superstition or to an occult interpretation of the number. The Bible teaches that there is no basis for attaching any superstitious powers to the number 666, or to any other number.

Jumping the Gun

Many have tried to figure out how near we are to the coming of Christ by identifying the Antichrist through numerical calculations. Such approaches will always fail and should not be attempted. Phone books are full of names that might add up. The wisdom of "counting the name" is not to be applied in our day, for that would be jumping the gun. Instead, it is to be applied by believers during the tribulation. As Daniel says, "These words are concealed and sealed up until the end time" (Daniel 12:9), referring, of course, to the tribulation period.

In 2 Thessalonians 2, Paul teaches that during the current church age the Antichrist is being restrained (verse 6).

Antichrist will not be "revealed" until "his time." The Holy Spirit's selection of the word revealed indicates that the identity of the Antichrist will be concealed until the time of his revelation at some point after the rapture. Thus, it is not possible to know or to figure out the identity of the Antichrist before "his time." What Paul has said explicitly is implied throughout Revelation. Revelation makes it clear, that, when the time comes, the identity of the Antichrist will be clear to believers. But until that time, people must resist what has been a popular prophetic pastime: naming the number.

As noted above, Revelation makes it clear that every believer during the tribulation will know that receiving the mark of the beast means rejecting Jesus Christ. This will be universally understood by Christians at the time. None of the suggestions of the past or any until the tribulation have merit.

Revelation 13:17,18 clearly says that the number 666 will be the mark proposed for the right hand or forehead. No one in history has even proposed such a number in anything like tribulation conditions, so past guesses as to his identity can also be nullified on this basis.

> The better part of wisdom is to be content that the identification is not yet available, but will be when the future false Christ ascends to his throne. The person to whom 666 applies must have been future to John's time, because John clearly meant the number to be recognizable to someone. If it was not discernible to his generation and those immediately following him—and it was not—the generation to whom it will be discernible must have lain (and still

lies) in the future. Past generations have provided many illustrations of this future personage, but all past candidates have proven inadequate as fulfillments.[7]

It is human nature to want to know more than God has revealed, but we must not start the race until the gun goes off.

Technology and the Mark

How does all of this relate to the coming cashless society? Perhaps the best way to show how it *does* relate is by first showing how it *does not* relate. The mark of the beast— 666—is not cashless technology or biometrics.

Some people have suggested that the mark of the beast will be a universal product code, a chip implanted under the skin, or an invisible mark that requires scanning technology to be recognized. Such applications do not align with what the Bible actually says. As we have seen, the Bible speaks clearly about what the mark will be. It will be:

- the Antichrist's mark, identified with his person
- the actual number 666, not a representation
- a mark, like a tattoo
- visible to the naked eye
- on you, not in you
- recognized, not questioned
- voluntary, not involuntary; thus not given apart from the person's knowledge
- used after the rapture, not before
- used in the second half of the tribulation
- needed to buy and sell

- universally received by non-Christians, but universally rejected by Christians
- a mark of worship and allegiance to the Antichrist
- promoted by the false prophet
- a definite sign that a person will face eternal punishment in the lake of fire

Probably no other number in history or in biblical studies has captivated the minds of both Christians and non-Christians as has "666." Even those who know nothing of the future plan of God as revealed in the Bible know there is significance to this number. Secular and religious writers, film makers, artists, and cultural critics allude to, portray, and expound upon it. It has been used and abused by evangelicals as well as by others, and it has been the subject of much fruitless speculation. Too often, sincere students of prophecy have tied the number to the potential of contemporary technology in an effort to demonstrate the relevance of their interpretation. Yet to do so is to put the "cart before the horse," for prophecy and the Bible do not gain authority or legitimacy because of culture or technology.

In summary, the technology of the coming cashless society will be used by the Antichrist, but it will not be used as the identifying mark of 666. Whatever technology is available at the time of the Antichrist's ascent will be used for evil purposes. It will be used by the Antichrist, in conjunction with the mark, to control buying and selling (as mentioned in Revelation 13:17), and it is likely that chip implants, scan technology, and biometrics will be used as tools to enforce his policy that one cannot buy or sell without the mark. As with other developments in our day, we see many trends setting the stage that will facilitate the future career of the Antichrist.

9

The Cashless Society

THE GOOD, THE BAD, AND THE UGLY

Is it possible that someday the dollar bill will be nothing more than a museum piece or that a generation of children will grow up without knowing the pleasure of change jingling in their pockets? In the future that looms ahead of us, that is not unthinkable. Interest in the cashless society is growing. Economists, theologians, computer engineers, sociologists, bankers, philosophers, and private citizens are all watching its development, but with mixed emotions. Each of these professional and vocational fields has advocates and detractors for a cashless society. The concerns are not only technological and philosophical, but also theological. There is much that needs to be discussed and evaluated: issues of privacy, freedom, and security. What will be the public and private consequences?

"Promised Land" or "No Man's Land"?

Are our technological developments cause for unrestricted celebration, or are there ramifications that should give us pause? In *Technopoly,* a stinging critique of technology's effect upon contemporary culture, Neil Postman recounts the history of the development of the clock, which had its origin in the Benedictine monasteries of the twelfth and thirteenth centuries. Originally designed to assist the monks in synchronizing times of prayer, those outside the monastery walls soon found uses for the clock, and it entered the larger society. But with these uses came some unintended negative consequences. He notes:

> The paradox, the surprise, and the wonder are that the clock was invented by men who wished to devote themselves more rigorously to God; it ended as the technology of greatest use to men who wished to devote themselves to the accumulation of money. In the eternal struggle between God and Mammon, the clock quite unpredictably favored the latter.[1]

As we consider the coming cashless society, what parallels might we see to Postman's words? Postman warns, "Unforeseen consequences stand in the way of all those who think they see clearly the direction in which a new technology will take us. Not even those who invent a technology can be assumed to be reliable prophets."[2]

Most observers see significant changes ahead for society. Futurist Edward Cornish writes:

> When steam engines first appeared in eighteenth-century Britain, no one dreamed that the curious contraptions were part of a sweeping historical transformation, now known as the Industrial Revolution. But we today have little doubt that computers and

telecommunications have brought a new revolution and that this new transformation will affect human life even more profoundly than its predecessor.[3]

But all the experts are not in agreement with Cornish. Cliff Stoll, an astronomer, computer whiz, and best-selling author on computer technology, believes the cashless society is overhyped. He argues that most people are as attached to real cash as he is. "I want money to go to the coffee shop to pay for a cup of coffee. I want money to pay my child an allowance. I want money in my pocket, real money—not credit-card money."[4] Consequently Stoll doesn't see much change on the horizon. "I feel the year 2025 won't be much different from the way it is today, just the way 1965 isn't much different from today."[5]

Better Safe Than Sorry

One reason observers such as Stoll are critical of technology and the cashless society is because of the many technical problems facing those who would implement it. Security and reliability are the two main concerns of those hesitant about the implementation of the cashless society. With funds being transferred from one account to another by the click of a button, how safe are they from manipulation and error? What safeguards would stop someone with computer know-how from initiating an illegal transfer of funds for personal gain?

Computer technology has created a new class of criminals, known as hackers, who pose a significant threat for the cashless society. Vast amounts of research and time are being spent in efforts to reduce the threat of computer criminals in the electronic-money marketplace. Companies such as GTE, IBM, Visa, and MasterCard are working closely together to develop standard software for assuring security of electronic payments over the Internet. Following a recent agreement between two credit-card giants, Edmund Jensen, CEO of Visa International, stated, "A single standard eliminates unnecessary costs and builds the case for doing business on the Internet." Eugene Lockhart, CEO for MasterCard, lauded the agreement, proclaiming the new standard as a "critical catalyst for electronic commerce."[6]

Other attempts at reducing theft are also in the works. ISED Corporation of New Jersey has developed a device that secures transactions over both the telephone and the Internet. Known as a SED (secure encryption device), this inexpensive instrument attaches either to a telephone or personal computer and is activated by running, or "swiping," an ATM or credit card through it. Account information encrypted on the magnetic stripe of the card is electronically transferred through the hardware. Reporting on the device's advent, CNN correspondent Marsha Walton writes:

> As buying by computer catches on, the device could eventually be used to pay for everything from a pizza delivery to bailing a friend out of jail, and would be as much a part of the home computer as a floppy disk or hard drive. And just as consumers have grown accustomed to computers and ATM cards, the combination of the two could be another step toward a "cashless society."[7]

In addition to the issue of security, there is also the concern for the reliability of the cashless system and its supporting hardware. The electronic systems must not only be secure from threats of internal tampering and theft, but they must also be resistant to external threats such as natural catastrophes, terrorism, or sabotage. Every possibility of the system "crashing" or being destroyed must be reduced as much as possible.

Precautions against such catastrophes have been considered and taken by at least one corporation, Visa International. In their headquarters in McLean, Virginia, the building that houses Visa's main computers has reportedly been constructed to withstand an earthquake equal to the magnitude of the 1906 San Francisco earthquake. The building has three power sources: the electric company, three diesel-powered backup generators, and two banks of lead-acid batteries similar to our automobile batteries.[8]

Advantages: The Good

What is it that makes electronic money, or e-money, so attractive? First, it may eventually be more convenient than traditional coins and currency. A 1994 *Time* magazine article reported that, as of 1994, almost one-fourth of all American homes had personal computers, and more than 900,000 subscribers had signed up with banking services via on-line information systems.[9]

Second, banks and other institutions using e-money would find it considerably cheaper to process than checks and other records. Regarding the high cost of processing checks, *Time* reported:

Checks too are expensive to handle. About 55 billion checks are written every year (more than 37% of all consumer payments), and the processing costs the nation's financial institutions about $1.30 each. Banks end up losing money on about half of all checking accounts, since the handling costs often exceed the interest earned on lending out the deposits. An electronic transfer, on the other hand, costs only 15 cents per blip.[10]

Cash is even harder and more costly to handle. Donald Gleason, president of the Smart Card Enterprise unit of Electronic Payment Services Inc., says:

Cash is a nightmare. It costs money handlers in the U.S. alone approximately $60 billion a year to move the stuff, a line item ripe for drastic pruning. The solution is to cram our currency in burn bags and strike some matches. This won't happen all at once, and paper money will probably never go away (hey, they couldn't even get rid of the penny), but bills and coinage will increasingly be replaced by some sort of electronic equivalent.[11]

Dollars wear out easier than electronic images. A cashless society would alleviate some of the headaches associated with keeping fresh currency in the marketplace.

A *Time* magazine article notes:

The push for a cashless society is gaining momentum, however, if only because making money disappear is also a way of saving money. There are about 12 billion pieces of U.S. paper

currency, worth $150 billion, circulating world-
wide, which works out to about $30 for every
person on earth. Keeping all that paper in use is a
costly chore for the government. Most $1 bills wear
out after about 18 months. To retire, destroy and
replace all aging currency costs the government an
estimated $200 million a year. Currency is cumber-
some for businesses as well. People have to count it,
armored cars have to carry it, bank vaults have to
store it and security guards have to protect it.[12]

A third advantage of electronic money is privacy. People
using the Internet for personal and business commercial
transactions may find that some forms of electronic money
offer greater privacy than current credit cards. But the potential certainly exists for privacy to be compromised in the
sphere of cyberspace.

A major advantage argued by proponents of the cashless
society is decreased crime. It has been estimated that in the
United States alone illegal transactions form an "under-
ground economy" that totals between 10 percent and 28 percent of the gross national product, and more than 50 percent
of these are done in cash.[13] A cashless society might be a significant deterrent to such activity:

> The immediate benefits would be profound and
> fundamental. Theft of cash would become impos-
> sible. Bank robberies and cash-register robberies
> would simply cease to occur. Attacks on shop-
> keepers, taxi drivers, and cashiers would all end.
> Purse snatchings would become a thing of the past.
> Urban streets would become safer. Retail shops in

once-dangerous areas could operate in safety. Security costs and insurance rates would fall. Property values would rise. Neighborhoods would improve.

Drug traffickers and their clients, burglars and receivers of stolen property, arsonists for hire, and bribe-takers would no longer have the advantage of using traceable currency. . . . Sales of illegal drugs, along with the concomitant violent crime, should diminish. Hospital emergency rooms would become less crowded. Burglary statistics would fall.[14]

Perhaps this scenario is overly optimistic, but many experts do believe that a cashless society is an important means of significantly decreasing certain types of crime. Of course, the possibility remains that these sorts of crimes would simply go high tech. To put too much hope in a cashless society reducing crime significantly seems unrealistic.

Disadvantages: The Bad

Granted, there are some advantages to not having to carry or use cash, but what's the other side of the coin?

We mentioned the possibility of an electronic system "crashing." If that happened, the ramifications could send economic shock waves around the world. Both institutions and individuals could be seriously affected. At worst, life savings and fortunes could be lost. At the very least, there would be significant anxiety and cessation of transactions until the systems could recover or backups restored. With no "paper trail," restoration or duplication of records could be an accountant's worst nightmare.

One vulnerable network of computers is Fedwire, which is run by the Federal Reserve and is the official network for clearing domestically issued checks. Also used by the Federal Reserve and Treasury Department, this system processes $1 trillion dollars on an average day.

Breakdowns are not unthinkable.... On November 21, 1985, a faulty software package kept the Bank of New York from receiving payments from customers. The bank paid its outstanding bills, but no money came in. By the time the error was detected late in the evening, the Bank of New York owed other banks on the Fedwire system 23 billion dollars.[15] This was just a "quick slip" of one part of the system, and yet it had enormous consequences. Joel Kurtzman writes:

> The Bank of New York had to raise a lot of money in a hurry. It had just one place to turn: the Fed. It was forced to borrow $23 billion overnight from the Fed until the problem was corrected the following morning. That money was lent to the Bank of New York at an overnight rate of about 5 percent—a little over $3.1 million in interest payments for the night.
>
> The problem affected just one bank on the network, but the imbalance was still huge. What would have happened if the bank's software problem had spread? Or if the problem had been caused deliberately by a virus inserted in the nation's bank-clearing system by a computer hacker or "financial terrorist"?[16]

A glitch like the one experienced by the Bank of New York could have unbelievable ripple effects. While safeguards

are being developed, the risk is still an ever-present danger.
Kurtzman says:

> The fact that Fedwire was not secure poses no
> small problem. With $1 trillion traveling through
> the system each day, a malfunction (accidental or
> otherwise) could paralyze the country. . . .
> In all there are twenty-one major electronic net-
> works around the world designed to move money.
> These systems move about $3 trillion a day. None of
> these systems is more secure or safer than Fedwire.
> Such are the perils of the information age.[17]

Disruption of these systems would create personal and
international chaos. If this can happen on a macroeconomic
level, how difficult would it be to interfere with one individual, or one family, or one group of people?

The Fedwire fiasco was a software problem, but what
happens when a typographical error enters the system? Just a
simple typo can also create chaos. At Chemical Bank in
1994, automated teller machines deducted $16 million dol-
lars by mistake from the accounts of 10,000 customers
because of a typographical error in a single line of computer
code. The result? The bank bounced 430 checks before the
error could be fixed.[18]

Another serious concern about the cashless society is that
it will further the distance between the economic haves and
have-nots. A cashless society assumes a certain level of economic and technological sophistication. Those with the
sophistication and access would benefit, and those without it
would not.

Potential: The Ugly

In addition to possible problems, there are some aspects of the cashless society that are downright ugly. Electronic footprints can be traced. When you make a credit-card purchase, the information becomes part of a much larger personal profile. Harvard legal scholar Anne Wells Branscomb writes:

> Far more pernicious than being submerged beneath a sea of catalogs, solicitations, and notices that you may have already won a million dollars is the compilation of data gathered from many sources, then correlated by computerized analysis to formulate profiles of our tastes, interests, and activities. This capability recalls the horror of George Orwell's novel 1984 in which Big Brother knows all about everyone and uses the exhaustive and reliable knowledge to manipulate their lives.[19]

On a macroeconomic level, there is the question of who is going to control the growth of electronic money systems. Will it be the public sector, the private sector, or the government?

Large-scale fraud is one of the greatest concerns facing the cashless society. Even with current technology, the Internal Revenue Service has reported that the number of fraudulent electronic filings has doubled in the last few years. *Time* magazine reported:

> Such incidents have led critics to warn that the rush to automated payment systems is proceeding too fast even for computer experts. "The demands

on software are far outpacing the development of software," says Dain Gary, a manager at the Software Engineering Institute at Carnegie-Mellon University.[20]

These concerns are real and the answers are not yet apparent. The cashless society will not transform the greed and the wayward desires of the human heart. Tax evasion, counterfeiting, theft, and money laundering will continue and could proliferate in a cashless society unless proper safeguards are developed. There are sizable regulatory gaps that currently "permit" electronic money laundering. These eventually need to be addressed. Stanley E. Morris, director of the Treasury Department's Financial Crimes Enforcement Network, reports that there are presently no laws that limit the balance of electronic currency that can be loaded onto an electronic cash card. This allows for great potential criminal activity and, so far, there is no way to define whose tax laws apply to transactions in cyberspace.[21]

Along these same lines, Steven Levy warns of the darker side of the cashless society:

> Exactly what goes on inside smart cards, wallets, and computers won't be apparent. But the protocols chosen by the lords of e-money are all-important. Depending on how they work, the various systems of electronic money will prove to be boons or disasters, bastions of individual privacy or violators of individual freedom. At the worst, a faulty or crackable system of electronic money could lead to an economic Chernobyl. Imagine the dark side: cryptocash hackers who figure out how to spoof an

e-money system. A desktop mint! The resulting flood of bad digits would make the hyper inflationary Weimer Republic—where people carted wheelbarrows full of marks to pay for groceries—look like a stable monetary system.[22]

Of even greater concern than the issues of fraud are those of control and privacy. Kawika Daguio, Washington, D.C., representative for the American Bankers Association, poses the following questions:

- "Who is going to create the monetary value?"
- "What security features will be included?"
- "Will they work so the value will be restored if they're lost?"
- "Who's going to regulate electronic money?"
- "Who's going to pay for it?"[23]

For each of these questions several different answers are being given and lots of heated discussion has erupted. How these questions are answered is of great importance to us all. But the greatest concern is controlling the system upon which the cashless society is built. Not everyone agrees that there will be centralized control or that such a thing is even possible. Many desire that it not be centralized. And so the pendulum of fear swings between a cashless society with too much governmental control and a cashless society with too little governmental control. Kurtzman expresses some of these concerns:

> And what about governments in this networked world? They have been downgraded when it comes

to running the economy. The trend that has been going on for more than a decade is for governments in every country to sell off their holdings and at the same time borrow more in the capital markets. . . . The power of government is decreasing at a rapid rate relative to the private sector. . . Government, business, commerce, and trade are all being redefined as globalization proceeds with dispatch.

The convergence of those two trends, a future more difficult to predict and government less able to act, is alarming. It may signal a future where there is too little central authority to stop a calamity before it occurs. The world may lack sufficient control mechanisms to curb chaos when it begins.[24]

Terrorism on the Internet is also a growing concern that is being addressed by the government. Jim Settle, retired director of the FBI's computer crime squad is very concerned: "You bring me a select group of hackers and within 90 days I'll bring this country to its knees."[25] Cyberterrorism is a personal, law enforcement, and national security issue for all of us.

It is not a matter of paranoid religious fanatics reading conspiracy into the cashless society equation. Rather, problems are inherent in the very concept. While we and others address the issues from a religious perspective, we are only one segment of those who have concerns and express them.

10

Knowledge, Power, and Privacy

SPEEDBUMPS ON THE INFORMATION HIGHWAY

T he trip to the mailbox these days is usually followed by an elaborate ritual of sorting out bills and correspondence from the proliferating array of advertisements, sweepstakes, catalogs and other forms of junk mail. Merchants have found that mass mailing to consumers are a cost-effective method of reaching potential buyers. But many consumers are frustrated by the growing numbers of unwanted mailings. Have you ever tried to get off the mailing lists of junk mail solicitors? It's not an easy task. How many people have access to your name and address and how did they get it? How many unsolicited calls for sales or contributions do you receive each week? Where did they get your number? These questions pose significant concerns about personal privacy and how easy it is for someone to "get the goods on us" so that they can peddle their goods to us.

So Much Information, So Many Decisions

Surfing the Internet can be overwhelming to the first-time user. It's exciting, and there's so much information available to us at the stroke of a key or the click of a mouse! But what do we do with all this information? The information highway is here to stay and it is growing, but like the highways we drive daily, it has the potential for disaster as well as convenience.

The amount of information available is phenomenal. With the option of putting many publications on a single CD-ROM, or visiting Internet sites around the world with the click of a button, the possibilities for accessing information are almost endless. In the end, the ethical questions surrounding this new technology concern how you use the information. Information is of little value unless it is applied. Clifford Stoll is right when he states, "Networks bring a flood of both useful and useless information to our desktops. They help me work more efficiently yet still are counterproductive—they're equally great for working and goofing off."[1]

Ups and Downs on the Highway

On the eve of the new millennium, computer technology has thrust us into a new world. In one critique of technology, Professor Albert Borgmann writes:

> Throughout modern history there has been the hope that happiness would burst forth from within technology, that science and ingenuity would design a device that would guarantee everyone's liberty and prosperity. The construction of the information highway has once more kindled that hope.[2]

Computer software magnate Bill Gates is one who has unbridled confidence in what the future holds. "I'm optimistic about the impact of the new technology,"[3] he says.

> We are watching something historic happen, and it will affect the world seismically, rocking us the same way the discovery of the scientific method, the invention of printing, and the arrival of the Industrial Age did. If the information highway is able to increase the understanding citizens of one country have about their neighboring countries, and thereby reduce international tensions, that, in and of itself, could be sufficient to justify the cost of implementation. If it was used only by scientists, permitting them to collaborate more effectively to find cures for the still-incurable diseases, that alone would be invaluable. If the system was only for kids, so that they could pursue their interests in and out of the classroom, that by itself would transform the human condition. The information highway won't solve every problem, but it will be a positive force in many areas.[4]

Understanding new technologies, especially those that increase our access to information, makes us keenly aware that this power can be harnessed, and that at times privacy will be compromised as a result. Because of what we know about biblical prophecy, Christians need to maintain both a posture that is optimistic, yet cautious. An uninhibited enthusiasm for the future makes society vulnerable to gross abuse and corruption.

The Perpetual Problem of Privacy

One of the intersections of the information highway, where computers and society merge, is privacy. It is a place of potential collision, and many people, frustrated by the threat or the delay in getting through, shout their views at one another. But everyone acknowledges the need to be concerned about privacy in the cybernetic world.

The difficulty is that present laws and regulations in countries throughout the world are inadequate for the issues we are now forced to face. Security does not always mean privacy, especially in the electronic world.

Observing the legal difficulties in Asia, one article states:

> The legal systems still have to catch up with technology. Though laws prescribe punishment for theft of money, the theft of information remains fuzzily defined, at least in Asia. The Malaysian Penal Code was drafted in 1936. "When our laws talk about theft, they refer to movable properties, not information," says law professor Khaw Lake Tee of the University of Malaya. "So how do you prosecute?"[5]

While the information age has alleviated some problems, it has also created others, one of which is the inadequacy of our laws. Everette E. Dennis, executive director of The Freedom Forum Media Studies Center at Columbia University, writes:

> What was once the stuff of graduate seminars on information theory or communications policy is now truly in the public arena, where it is beginning to dawn on people that the information revolution

may affect them in helpful or harmful ways. In part, the message here is that what you don't know or don't protect can make your life quite perilous.[6]

Who owns your telephone number? What about your e-mail? How private are your medical records? How public should records of your financial transactions be, and who should be able to access them? And where does the government (at any level or location) fit into the privacy equation? All of these are standard legal questions that are compounded in complexity by computer technology and telecommunications.

There is a major speed bump in the information highway in regard to privacy. Observing some of the new legal dilemmas, Anne Wells Branscomb writes:

> No information society will reach its potential without addressing the legal foundation upon which information is exchanged. That foundation is as necessary a component of the information infra-structure or "infostructure" as the electronic global highways that we are rapidly constructing. The boundaries between what is considered to be public information and what is considered to be private have been moving targets for several generations now. Unless we are able to reach a consensus on the fair uses and prohibited abuses of information, we will never achieve the promise of living in an information society.[7]

Between a Rock and a Hard Place

The issues of privacy are positioned on a large philosophical pendulum. At one end of the arc there are the advocates of complete anonymity in cashless society transactions. But this opens the door to possibilities of abuse that may as yet be unknown. No matter what laws are enacted, the unscrupulous will always be looking for an advantage. At the other end of the arc is the extreme position of complete identification and traceability. Few people in our society would advocate this position.

Steven Levy writes of the dilemma of privacy:

> If anonymity becomes a standard in cyberspace cash systems, we have to accept its potential abuse— as in copyright violations, fraud, and money laundering. Innovative new crypto schemes have the potential for mitigating these abuses, but the fact of anonymity guarantees that some skullduggery will be easier to pull off. On the other hand, the lack of anonymity means that every move you make, and every file you take, will be traceable. That opens the door to surveillance like we've never seen.[8]

These are the concerns that people like David Chaum voice. We can't have it both ways. "In one direction lies unprecedented scrutiny and control of people's lives; in the other, secure parity between individuals and organizations. The shape of society in the next century may depend on which approach predominates.[9]

Convenience or Control?

The ability to gather vast amounts of information leads to the question of what information should become open or public and what should remain closed or private. How much should other people, institutions, or governments be allowed to know about you and your activities? What are the boundaries and safeguards, and who will decide?

The amount of information someone has about you is certainly a factor in determining how much control the person exerts over you. Information, like technology, can be used for good or for evil. Privacy is the door through which power must pass to access information about our lives. Once that door is completely opened, we become vulnerable to manipulation and control. Futurist author Alvin Toffler believes that the control of knowledge "is the crux of tomorrow's worldwide struggle for power in every human institution."[10] Russell Chandler, former religion editor for *The Los Angeles Times,* sees an ominous potential for technology, power, and privacy:

> While we consider these technological wonders beckoning us to cross the threshold of 2001, it's essential that we grasp both the limitations and the potential for subversion inherent in technology. Information-hungry technology in a high-surveillance society can erode our freedoms and compromise our privacy. . . . If worshipped, technology in the end proves to be a false god, corroding human values and desensitizing the spirit. . . . The siren song of "liberation technology" conceals the negative consequences of technical progress in contemporary society.[11]

While some cultural critics and political observers have expressed an unbridled optimism that democratic ideals will soon gallop around the globe, others are more constrained in their evaluations. In his book *Has Democracy Had Its Day?*

theologian Carl F. H. Henry expresses some of the concerns about the survival of democracy that have been growing in the minds of conservatives and evangelicals in the last few years. He offers words of hope, but also words of caution:

> Nothing has threatened the survival of modern political democracy more than Marxist communism. One might expect that the collapse of communism in our time would evoke for democratic political processes a torrent of international tribute, yet we are seeing instead a rising tide of doubt precisely at this time.
>
> The questioning of democracy occurs for different reasons in Latin America, in Asia, and even in Russia and Eastern Europe. But most astonishing, it appears more and more frequently in the United States, in the aftermath of the cultural loss of moral transcendence and of the privatization of religion.[12]

Although a cashless society offers welcomed convenience for all, our concern is its potential for unprecedented control of individuals and of society as a whole. So where does this leave us in relation to the information highway? Should we refuse to use it because there may be hurdles to overcome? Certainly not. There is much to be gained from its use, and we encourage you to become as familiar as possible with it. But like the automobiles we drive, we need to be alert to what is going on around us. Not all roads lead to the same place, and there are some places we don't want to go.

Because we firmly believe the Bible and its prophetic teachings, we see that there is cause for concern about the potential uses of technology. An understanding of the Bible and the world view it presents certainly does not forbid the use of technology. But we must be aware of its potential. The technology that we see and use today may be used for evil in the near future. That which is intended for good is, at some point, always in danger of being abused and corrupted by the human heart.

11

Will Technology Bring Us a Better World?

HINDRANCE, HOPE, AND HYPE

Both the authors grew up in Texas where the summer sun beats down mercilessly, and no one appreciates air conditioning more than we do. This marvelous technology, which allows us to moderate our indoor temperature when the thermometer outside soars above 100 degrees, makes us much more comfortable. But are we "better" in an ethical and moral sense because of it? Probably not, except that we may not be quite so cranky in the summer. Are we "better" in a theological sense because of air conditioning? Absolutely not. We still have a sin nature, which climate control will do nothing to alter. In fact, because of our sinful nature, the multiplication of new technologies is often used by people as a diversion from dealing with more important questions of spirituality and morality. Too frequently we'd rather be amused with our new technological toys than consider the timeless issues relating to the human condition.

Technology in itself is not evil. The crucial question has to do with how technology is used. An automobile in the hands of a drunk driver can kill many people, but an ambulance in the hands of a skillful driver can save many lives. The syringe, designed to be used by nurses and physicians to inject medicine to heal, can also be used by drug addicts to destroy their own lives. It is the application of an individual technology not its presence or development that is often wrong.

Sometimes, You Can't Win for Losing

Many of the advances propelling us toward the cashless society are good in themselves. But what may begin as good, may be corrupted and used for evil ends. We have examined legitimate concerns regarding privacy, theft, and the difficulty of coping with the information explosion, as well as what the Bible says about future events. We are daily being drawn closer to earth's final days, and even now, the world is being conditioned to facilitate the ascent of the Antichrist.

Because we are sinful and self-serving, anything that we create and develop, whether it is art or architecture, music or machines, electronics or eugenics can be, and eventually will be distorted and misapplied. Theologian Carl F. H. Henry keenly notes of our contemporary society:

> Much of the West, although technocratically pre-occupied with the *what* of things may seem to have lost interest in the *why*. But the *why* is what continually confronts us, even Christians, not only through the human dilemmas of pain and evil but also and especially through the Bible where the

living God of revelation searches the thoughts and
intents of the heart.[1]

As we noted in the first chapter, the problem of evil is not
an issue of technology but of theology. We are not to be
afraid of technology or avoid it. Rather, we are to be aware of
how it might be used and we are to wisely evaluate these uses
and the moral and ethical boundaries of our participation.
Just because we have the ability to do something doesn't
mean we should do it.

Because people want to avoid their responsibility to God,
inherent in creation, they want to shift the blame. This was
the original response to sin in the Garden by Adam and Eve
and its popularity has not abated. In our day, people often
misassign evil to that which is not responsible. Guns,
poverty, crime, technology, industrialization, and hectic
lifestyles, to name only a few, instead of people whose actions
are the true source of social and environmental realities. Yet,
if everyone was capable of candid thought, we would all
admit that machines cannot make ethical decisions. Even the
most advanced computer can only function according to its
programs. It must be clear that men and women through
their decisions and actions are the only agents who can put a
moral imprint on anything. It is humanity that will lead to
Armageddon, not armor.

Technology is carrying us to new frontiers in many areas
of our lives and therefore we need to continually critique our
culture and society from a biblical perspective. Not all
"progress" is morally and ethically desirable. There may be
some technologies that Christians, individually, decide they
should not use because to do so would violate biblical

principles. For example, a person's view on theological issues relating to the beginning and ending of life may limit use of medical technology. We must know what we believe, why we believe it, and what the ramifications of those beliefs are to be in our actions.

A Preview of Coming Attractions

The bottom line on the cashless society is not that it is immoral or evil, but that it is a sign of the end times. Before the feature film is shown in a cinema there are frequently several previews of upcoming films shown to entice you to return and watch them. In much the same way, the cashless society is a preview or glimpse of life in the future. Unfortunately, the feature production will exceed any horror film known today. It will be a seven-year tribulation following the rapture of the church and the major "star" will be the Antichrist. The cashless society is only one aspect of his overall plan and today's technology.

It would, however, be wrong to think that because something may or will be used for evil in the future, we should therefore avoid it or resolutely reject its use in the present. The cashless society is coming and the tribulation is coming. But the Lord Jesus Christ is also coming for His own before the terrors of the tribulation come to fruition. We encourage our readers to consider first and foremost the consequences of living with a Christless soul rather than the consequences of living in a cashless society. "For what will it profit a man if he gains the whole world and forfeits his soul? Or what will a man give in exchange for his soul" (Matthew 16:26).

12

The Bottom Line

The second coming of Jesus Christ will bring an end to the seven-year tribulation and reign of the Antichrist. After His return, Jesus Christ will commence His righteous reign of 1000 years, known as the millennial kingdom. The prophetic words regarding a new covenant, to be written by God on the hearts of His people (Jeremiah 31:31-34) during the millennium, will be a vivid contrast to the mark the followers of the Antichrist will bear. Finally, the prayer that has been voiced to God the Father since Christ first taught it to His disciples will be fully realized at the outset of the millennial kingdom. The words "Thy kingdom come. Thy will be done, on earth as it is in heaven" will be no more than the memory of a longing now fully satisfied. The Antichrist will be destroyed, and Jesus Christ will rule in righteous benevolence. The terrors of the tribulation will give way to the majesty of the millennium.[1]

The safety and security that non-Christians will seek in accepting the Antichrist and his program is a false security and a false salvation. It may bring temporary physical and economic security, or even affluence, but it will not last. This false security stands in stark contrast to that which the redeemed of God will experience in the millennial kingdom. The plans and programs of the tribulation are economically, experientially, and in every other way truly "anti-Christ." The deceptions of the Antichrist are as evil and destructive as the salvation offered by Jesus Christ is compassionate and forgiving.

Bust and Boom:
The Tribulation and the Millennium

We have already studied extensively the tribulation era. But what about the millennium? Numerous Old Testament passages speak of a yet-future time of true peace and prosperity for the righteous followers of God under the benevolent physical rule of Jesus Christ on the earth. Zechariah 14:9 speaks of this time saying, "And the LORD will be king over all the earth; in that day the LORD will be the *only* one, and His name the *only* one." The passage continues in verses 16-21 to describe some of the millennial conditions. Even though the Bible speaks descriptively throughout the Old Testament about the millennial kingdom, it is not until the final book—Revelation—that the length of His kingdom is revealed (Revelation 20:2-7).

Isaiah also foretold this future era. In his prophecy, given 700 years before the birth of Jesus Christ, he declared:

Now it will come about that in the last days, the mountain of the house of the LORD will be established as the chief of the mountains, and will be raised above the hills; and all the nations will stream to it. And many peoples will come and say, "Come, let us go up to the mountain of the LORD, To the house of the God of Jacob; that He may teach us concerning His ways, and that we may walk in His paths." For the law will go forth from Zion, and the word of the LORD from Jerusalem. And He will judge between the nations, and will render decisions for many peoples; and they will hammer their swords into plowshares, and their spears into pruning hooks. Nation will not lift up sword against nation, and never again will they learn war (Isaiah 2:2-4).

Several chapters later, Isaiah again writes of the millennium:

And the wolf will dwell with the lamb, and the leopard will lie down with the kid, and the calf and the young lion and the fatling together; and a little boy will lead them. Also the cow and the bear will graze; Their young will lie down together; and the lion will eat straw like the ox. And the nursing child will play by the hole of the cobra, and the weaned child will put his hand on the viper's den. They will not hurt or destroy in all My holy mountain, For the earth will be full of the knowledge of the LORD as the waters cover the sea (Isaiah 11:6-9).

Other extensive Old Testament passages about the millennium include Psalm 2:6-9; Isaiah 65:18-23; Jeremiah

31:12-14,31-37; Ezekiel 34:25-29; 37:1-6; 40-48; Daniel 2:35; 7:13,14; Joel 2:21-27; Amos 9:13,14; Micah 4:1-7; and Zephaniah 3:9-20. (These are only a few of scores of prophetic passages regarding the millennium.) Prophecy scholar David Larsen summarizes these texts succinctly, noting, "The whole bulk of Old Testament prophecy points to the establishment of a kingdom of peace upon earth when the law will go forth from Mount Zion."[2]

The millennial kingdom will bring about harmony in all of creation, for every area of lives will be changed for the better. In Isaiah chapters 11 and 35, the prophet provides extensive comment on the physical aspects of the kingdom.

Ever since the fall of Adam and Eve, humanity and creation have been under the judgment of their original sin. Sin's influence on humanity and on all of creation is immeasurable. Because of the fall, the ground was cursed and the necessity of working to acquire food, clothing, and shelter created a competitive atmosphere in which the development of money, bartering, and other commercial transactions became commonplace.

The apostle Paul reminds us of the turmoil of our premillennial experience: "For we know that the whole creation groans and suffers the pains of childbirth together until now" (Romans 8:22). However, during the millennium there will be a partial lifting of the curse and the ramifications of original sin.

In Isaiah 35:1,2, we read of some of the effects of the millennium on the environment:

> The wilderness and the desert will be glad, and
> the Arabah will rejoice and blossom; like the crocus

it will blossom profusely and rejoice with rejoicing and shout of joy. The glory of Lebanon will be given to it, the majesty of Carmel and Sharon. They will see the glory of the LORD, the majesty of our God.

There will be abundant rainfall in areas that today are known for their dryness. Food for human consumption and for livestock will be plentiful:

Then He will give you rain for the seed which you will sow in the ground, and bread from the yield of the ground, and it will be rich and plenteous; on that day your livestock will graze in a roomy pasture. Also the oxen and the donkeys which work the ground will eat salted fodder, which has been winnowed with shovel and fork (Isaiah 30:23,24).

And the scorched land will become a pool, and the thirsty ground springs of water; in the haunt of jackals, its resting place, grass becomes reeds and rushes (Isaiah 35:7).

As part of nature and the created order, animal life will also be affected. Predatory instincts and carnivorous appetites will cease in animals. The distinctions between "tame" and "wild" will be erased as all creatures will live in harmony (Isaiah 11:6,7). Physical conditions for people will also be drastically changed for the better. Just as in the days before the flood in the time of Noah, people will live much longer, and the birthrate will increase again since the tribulation will be completed:

No longer will there be in it an infant who lives but a few days, or an old man who does not live out his days; for the youth will die at the age of one hundred and the one who does not reach the age of one hundred shall be thought accursed (Isaiah 65:20).

O people in Zion, inhabitant in Jerusalem, you will weep no longer. He will surely be gracious to you at the sound of your cry; when He hears it, He will answer you. Although the Lord has given you bread of privation and water of oppression, He, your Teacher will no longer hide Himself, but your eyes will behold your Teacher (Isaiah 30:19,20).

Additionally, many physical infirmities and health concerns will be eradicated:

And on that day the deaf shall hear words of a book, and out of their gloom and darkness the eyes of the blind shall see (Isaiah 29:18).

And no resident will say, "I am sick"; the people who dwell there will be forgiven their iniquity (Isaiah 33:24).

In the midst of this enhanced environment and increased level of health, the overall effect will be increased prosperity as poverty, injustice, and disease cease. Jeremiah describes the prosperity that citizens of the millennial kingdom will experience:

"And they shall come and shout for joy on the height of Zion, and they shall be radiant over the bounty of the LORD—over the grain, and the new wine, and the oil, and over the young of the flock and the herd; and their life shall be like a watered garden, and they shall never languish again. Then the virgin shall rejoice in the dance, and the young men and the old, together, for I will turn their mourning into joy, and will comfort them, and give them joy for their sorrow. And I will fill the soul of the priests with abundance, and My people shall be satisfied with My goodness," declares the LORD (Jeremiah 31:12-14).

The physical conditions of the millennium will be tremendous. There will be widespread peace and justice and spiritual blessings will also be abundant. There will be an abundance of food and economic property. Because there is justice, problems such as the unequal distribution of goods, labor disputes, and poverty will subside. It will truly be a magnificent era (Isaiah 65:21-25; Joel 2:21-27; Amos 9:13-14).[3]

Unfortunately, even in the midst of such pristine conditions, there will ultimately be human rebellion. Because the complete effects of the fall will not be erased, there will be a final revolt against the righteous government of Jesus Christ. This will occur at the end of the millennium when Satan is briefly released from bondage just prior to his final judgment and destruction (Revelation 20:7-10). Dr. Walvoord observes:

> Taken as a whole, the social and economic conditions of the millennium indicate a golden age in which the dreams of social reformists through the centuries will be realized, not through human effort but by the immediate presence and power of God and the righteous government of Christ. That mankind should again fail under such ideal circumstances and be ready to rebel against Christ at the

end of the millennium is the final answer to those
who put faith in the inherent goodness of man.[4]

Prophetic Living Today

As we watch the news, read the papers, and consider our
own lives, we often wonder if the world is about to experience the dawning of a new age, or if it is facing the eve of
destruction. The Bible has the answer and will serve as our
guide if we permit it to do so. It will also serve as our critic.
Dr. Henry has rightly observed:

> The Bible is still the most incisive critic of our
> age. It confronts our broken love of God, our dull
> sense of justice, our shameful moral nakedness, our
> waning sense of ethical duty, our badly numbed
> consciences, our clutching anxieties, the ghastly hor-
> rors and brutal violence of this era.[5]

Our hope for the future rests firmly in the person and
work of Jesus Christ and in His return. There is, literally, a
world of difference between reaching for your pocketbook
and reaching for your Bible. One brings temporal rewards,
the other, eternal rewards. We encourage Christian readers to
remember that, as Christians, our primary concern is not the
coming cashless society, but the reality of a present Christless
society. Though the ethical concerns of a cashless society
need to be understood and addressed by Christians, their
importance fades in light of the worldview and evangelistic
responsibilities connected with the imminent return of
Christ.

Dollars and Sense

A story is told about a rich old man with a miserable disposition. One day he visited a rabbi, who led him to a window.

"Look out there," he said, and the rich man looked into the street.

"What do you see?" asked the rabbi.

"I see men, women, and children," answered the rich man.

Again the rabbi took him by the hand and this time led him to a mirror.

"Now what do you see?" asked the rabbi.

"Now I see myself," the rich man replied.

Then the rabbi said, "Behold, in the window there is glass, and in the mirror there is glass. But the glass of the mirror is covered with a little silver, and no sooner is the silver added than you cease to see others, but see only yourself."

What is true of "seeing others" in this story is also true about seeing God. Money, whether electronic or paper, digital or dollars, can bring us to the place where we no longer see Him, but only ourselves.

In our present society, as well as in a potential cashless society, money will buy a bed, but not rest; food, but not satisfaction; luxury, but not contentment; stocks, but not security; a house, but not a home; sedatives, but not a Savior. "Would it not be high tragedy if our affluent society collapsed into unexpected bankruptcy because, by exploring one world only, it lost the real world of tomorrow and the enduring world of eternity?"[6] What money cannot buy, God offers without charge. Making dollars and making sense are sometimes two very different things. Jesus offered us an interesting challenge in perspective and priority when He asked, "For what does it profit a man to gain the whole world, and forfeit his soul?" (Mark 8:36).

13

No Fear
of the Future

IF YOU ARE PREPARED

*"The intellectual suppression of God in His
revelation has precipitated the bankruptcy of a
civilization that turned its back on heaven only
to make its bed in hell."* [1]

—Carl F. H. Henry

Perhaps you have reached this final chapter and yet do
not know for sure what your eternal destiny will be.
If so, then this is the most important chapter of the book for
you, and we encourage you to carefully consider its contents.

Throughout this volume we have focused upon John's
book of Revelation. God used him to write another portion
of the Bible, known as the Gospel of John. Near the end of
John's Gospel, he writes, "These [things] have been written
that you may believe that Jesus is the Christ, the Son of God;
and that believing you may have life in His name" (John
20:31). We would like you to know for sure that you have
eternal life through Jesus Christ, God's Son.

In Revelation, a last invitation is issued: "And the Spirit and the bride say, 'Come.' And let the one who hears say, 'Come.' And let the one who is thirsty come; let the one who wishes take the water of life without cost" (Revelation 22:17). What does this invitation mean?

The image is that of a wedding. The groom has issued an invitation to the bride. The groom is willing, but is the bride willing? God has made provision, at no expense to you but at great expense to Him, for you to enter into a relationship with Him that will give you eternal life. More specifically, the invitation is issued to the one who hears and who is thirsty. Those familiar with the language of Scripture know that "thirst" represents a need. This need is forgiveness of sin. Thus, you must recognize that you are a sinner in the eyes of God: "For all have sinned and fall short of the glory of God" (Romans 3:23). God is holy and thus cannot ignore anyone's sin. He must judge it. However, God in His mercy has provided a way by which sinful men and women can receive His forgiveness. This forgiveness was provided at a great cost by Jesus Christ when He came to earth 2000 years ago, lived a perfect life, and died on the cross in our place to pay for our sin: "For the wages of sin is death, but the free gift of God is eternal life in Jesus Christ our Lord" (Romans 6:23). The Bible also says, "Christ died for our sins according to the Scriptures, and that He was buried, and that He was raised on the third day according to the Scriptures" (1 Corinthians 15:3,4).

In order to obtain this salvation and eternal life that Jesus Christ offers, we must individually trust that Christ's payment through His death on the cross is the only way that we can receive the forgiveness of our sins, the reestablishment of a relationship with God, and eternal life. "For by grace you have been saved through faith; and that not of yourselves, it is the gift of God; not as a result of works, that no one should boast" (Ephesians 2:8,9). This is why John invites the thirsty to come and enter into a relationship with God through Christ.

Are you thirsty? Do you recognize your sin before God? If you do, then come to Christ. If you do not acknowledge your need for salvation, then you by pass this opportunity. Please don't.

Those who are thirsty and want salvation can express their trust through the following prayer:

> Dear Lord,
> I know that I have done wrong and fallen short of Your perfect ways. I realize that my sins have separated me from You and that I deserve Your judgment. I believe that You sent Your Son, Jesus Christ, to earth to die on the cross for my sins. I put my trust in Jesus Christ and what He did on the cross as payment for my sins. Please forgive me and give me eternal life. Amen.

If you just prayed this prayer in sincerity, you are now a child of God and have eternal life. As His child you will want to develop this wonderful relationship by learning more about God through study of the Bible. You will want to find a church that teaches God's Word, encourages fellowship with other believers, and promotes the spreading of God's message of forgiveness to others.

If you were a Christian before reading this book, we encourage you to continue in your relationship with Christ. As you grow, you will want to live for Him in light of His coming. You will want to continue to spread the message of forgiveness which you have experienced. As you see God setting the stage for the end-time drama of the tribulation this should motivate you to increased service until He comes. May your heart be occupied with His words:

> Behold, I am coming quickly, and My reward is with Me, to render to every man according to what he has done. I am the Alpha and the Omega, the first and the last, the beginning and the end." Blessed are those who wash their robes, that they may have the right to the tree of life, and may enter by the gates into the city (Revelation 22:12-14).

APPENDIX

Tracking the Cashless Society on the Internet

As we started researching this book, we were uncertain how much material we would find on the topic of the cashless system. A couple of hours on the Internet resolved that problem but created another one—information overload! The addresses below are some the sites we visited or came across in our research. Their significance for this volume varies, but all have at least some relationship to our topic. Some are commercial sites and vendors, some are organizations, associations, and institutions. If you are interested in tracking developments of the growing cashless society, these addresses will get you started. Listing does not in any way denote agreement with the goals or information found at the site.

Some of the Major Digital Systems and Digital Money Vendors

Check free
http://www.checkfree.com

CyberCash
http://www.cybercash.com

DigiCash
http://www.digicash.com/index.html

First Virtual Holdings
   http://www.fv.com

Netscape Communications
   http://mosaic.mcom.com

Open Market, Inc.
   http://www.openmarket.com

Mondex
   http://www.mondex.com/mondex/home.html

Surety [Digital Notary (tm) System]
   http://www.surety.com

Netchex
   http://www.netchex.com

Global Village Bank
   gvb@aol.com

NetBank
   netbank-info@agents.com
   http://www.netbank,com/~netcash/

Legal Organizations With Cashless Society Interests

Electronic Frontier Foundation
   http://www.eff.org

Computer Professionals for Social Responsibility
   cpsr@cpsr.org

Electronic Privacy Information Center
   http://epic.digicash.com/epic
   http://cpsr.org/cpsr/privacy/epic

Other Organizations and Institutions

The Conditional AccesS for Europe Project (CAFE Project)
E-mail: cafe@cwi.nl

Certification for Electronic Commerce (CEC)
http://www.batnet.com/trac.html

Congressional Web Site
http://thomas.loc.gov

Biometric Information and Resource Sites

The Biometric Consortium
http://www.vitro.bloomington.in.us:8080/~bc?

Biometrics Journal Home Page
BJournal@cubbs.comm

AfB Biometrics HomePage
http://www.npl.co.uk/~dsg/afb.html

Automatic I.D. News
AutoID@en.com

Bar Code Home Page
http://mgfx.com

Smart Card Technology

Visa
http://www.visa.com/visa/Future.html

MasterCard
http://www.mastercard.com/Vision/smart.htm

AT&T
http://www.att.com

Motorola
http://www.motorola.com

IBM
http://www.ibm.com

News and Research Services

Electronic Telegraph
et@telegraph.co.uk

CNN
http://www.cnn.com

NlightN(TM)
http://www.nlightn.com

USA Today
http://www.usatoday.com

New York Times
http://www.nyt.com

Wall Street Journal
http://www.wsj.com

RAM Research Group
http://www.ramresearch.com/choices/html
http://www.ramresearch.com/cgi-bin/cardsearch

NOTES

CHAPTER 1

1. Bill Gates, *The Road Ahead* (New York: Penguin Books, 1995), p. 276.

2. Unabomber [pseudonym], "Industrial Society and Its Future, 1995, taken from the Internet.

3. Don Tapscott, *The Digital Economy: Promise and Peril in the Age of Networked Intelligence* (New York: McGraw-Hill, 1995), p. xiii.

CHAPTER 2

1. Simson Garfield, "The Road Watches You," *The New York Times*, May 3, 1995, A-15.1.

2. "Why One Olympic Debut Could Change How You Carry Cash," *Money*, June 1996,
pp. 55-56.

3. "Snapshot" Internet Edition, *USA Today*, n.d.

4. Ibid.

5. Cable Network News Home Page (Internet), "Why Wait in Line When You Can Shop On-Line?" September 26, 1995.

6. Steven Levy, "E-Money (That's What I Want)," unpublished paper (1996), p. 2, from the Internet .

7. AT&T News Release, "AT&T to License Smart Card Technology for Cashless Transactions," May 31, 1995, from the Internet.

8. Ricardo Saludo with Assif Shameen, "Ruler of Our Lives?" *AsiaWeek*, November 3, 1995, p. 2, from the Internet.

9. AT&T News Release, "AT&T and GiroVend Agree to Promote Smart Card Applications," January 18, 1995, from the Internet.

10. "Cashless in Hainan," *AsiaWeek*, November 3, 1995, p. 2, from the Internet.

11. Saludo, p. 3.

12. "UK Opens National ID Debate," *Government Technology*, August, 1995, quoted by Terry L. Cook, *The Mark of the New World Order* (Indianapolis, IN: Virtue International Pub., 1996), p. 544. While the authors are not in complete agreement with all of Cook's writing, it is a helpful and comprehensive presentation.

13. Thomas Sowell, "Liberals, Conservatives on Immigration," *Honolulu Star-Bulletin*, June 24, 1995, quoted by Cook, ibid., p. 541.

14. Don Tapscott, *The Digital Economy: Promise and Peril in the Age of Networked Intelligence* (New York: McGraw-Hill, 1995), pp. 45-46.

179

CHAPTER 3

1. "Cybersafety First," *AsiaWeek*, November 3, 1995, from the Internet.

2. "Electronic Money: So much for the Cashless Society/*The Economist*, November 26, 1994, p. 22

3. Ibid.

4. Ibid.

5. Daniel C. Lynch and Leslie Lundquist, *Digital Money: The New Era of Internet Commerce* (New York: John Wiley & Sons, 1996), p. 99. This is an excellent overview of digital money, written to give business executives a summary and easy reference guide.

6. Ibid.

7. Ibid., pp. 108-09.

8. Bill Gates, *The Road Ahead* (New York: Penguin Books, 1995), pp. 74-75.

9. David R. Warwick, "The Cash-Free Society," *The Futurist*, November-December 1992, p. 20.

10. "DigiCash—Numbers That Are Money," DigiCash company information publication, from the Internet.

11. David Chaum, "Achieving Electronic Privacy," *Scientific American*, August 1992, pp. 96-101.

12. Steven Levy, "E-Money (That's What I Want)," unpublished paper (1996), p. 2, from the Internet.

13. "Electronic Money," p. 22.

14. Ibid.

15. Ibid.

16. Ibid. For more detailed and technical explanations see Levy's "E-Money" paper or DigiCash's "Digicash—Numbers That Are Money."

17. Levy, p. 10.

18. Joel Kurtzman, *The Death of Money* (Boston: Little, Brown & Co., 1993), pp. 166-67.

19. Ibid., p. 170.

CHAPTER 4

1. See, for example, Robert A. Hendrickson's *The Cashless Society* (New York: Dodd, Mead & Co., 1972).

2. Glyn Davies, *A History of Money from Ancient Times to the Present Day* (Cardiff: University of Wales Press, 1994), p. 646. Quotation taken from the Internet, Home Page by Roy Davies, "Democracy and Government Control of the Money Supply," p. 1.

3. Michael A. Ramirez, "Towards a Cashless Society," unpublished paper (1993), p. 1, acquired from the author's Home Page on the Internet. Mr. Ramirez provides a

good summary of the cashless society. See the bibliography and appendix for additional information.

4. Ibid., p. 3.

5. "Electronic Money: So Much for the Cashless Society," *The Economist*, November 26, 1994, p. 23.

6. Levy, "E-Money (That's What I Want)," unpublished paper (1996), p. 1, from the Internet.

7. Joel Kurtzman, *The Death of Money* (Boston: Little, Brown & Co., 1993), p. 13.

8. Ibid., p. 11.

9. Ibid., p. 19.

10. Ibid.

11. Edward Cornish, "The Cyber Future: 92 Ways Our Lives Will Change by the Year 2025," Bethesda, MD: World Future Society, 1996, p. 10.

12. Ibid.

13. Kurtzman, p. 17.

14. Thomas McCarroll, "No Checks. No Cash. No Fuss?" *Time*, May 9, 1994, vol. 143, no. 19, from the Internet.

15. Ibid.

16. Comtex Scientific Corporation, "A Cashless Society Could be in Our Future," Knight-Ridder Wire Services, December 15, 1994, from the Internet.

17. Ibid.

18. David R. Warwick, "The Cash-Free Society," *The Futurist*, November-December, 1992, p. 20.

19. Kurtzman, p. 15.

20. Ibid., p. 16.

21. Ibid.

22. Warwick, p. 22.

23. Ibid., p. 20.

24. Ibid.

25. Albert Borgmann, "The Meaning of Technology," *The World & I*, March 1996, p. 289.

26. Carl Mitchum, "Techonology and Ethics: From Expertise to Public Participation," *The World I*, March 1996, p. 329.

CHAPTER 5

1. "Biometric Systems Suit Many Areas," *Automatic I.D. News*, August 1994, p. 20.

2. John Burnell, "A Defaced Face Can't Beat the Heat," *Automatic I.D. News*, July 1995, pp. 1, 18.

3. Cable Network News, "You Can't Leave Home Without It," December 7, 1995, from the Internet.

4. Cf. "RF/ID Pet Tagging Standard May Be Finalized This Year," and "RF/ID-Based Car Security System Offered," *Automatic I.D. News,* March 1995, pp. 14 and 20 respectively.

5. Sematech News Release, "0.35 Micron: Gateway to Talking Computers, Home Medicine & More," January 21, 1993.

6. Kathleen Wiegner, "Giving Surgical Implants IDs," *Los Angeles Times,* August 17, 1994, quoted by Terry L. Cook, *The Mark of the New World Order* (Indianapolis, IN: Virtue International Pub., 1996), p. 594.

7. Edward Cornish, "The Cyber Future: 92 Way Our Lives Will Change by the Year 2025," Bethesda, MD: World Future Society, 1996, p.2.

8. Martin Anderson, "High-Tech National Tattoo," *The Washington Times,* October 11, 1993, reprinted in Cook, p. 621.

CHAPTER 6

1. Carl. F.H. Henry, *Carl Henry at His Best* (Portland, OR: Multnomah Press, 1989), p. 128.

2. Charles C. Ryrie, *The Final Countdown* (Wheaton, IL: Victor Books, 1982), p. 7.

3. For an excellent overview of the rapture see Thomas Ice and Timothy Demy, *The Truth About the Rapture* (Eugene, OR: Harvest House, 1996).

4. For a more thorough treatment of these passages, see J. Randall Price, "Old Testament Tribulation Terms," in *When the Trumpet Sounds,* eds. Thomas Ice and Timothy Demy (Eugene, OR: Harvest House, 1995), pp. 57-84.

5. For an overview of the tribulation see Thomas Ice and Timothy Demy, *The Truth About the Tribulation* (Eugene, OR: Harvest House, 1996).

6. For a complete overview of current efforts to rebuild Israel's Temple see Thomas Ice and Randall Price, *Ready to Rebuild: The Imminent Plan to Rebuild the Last Days' Temple* (Eugene, OR: Harvest House, 1992), or Thomas Ice and Timothy Demy, *The Truth About the Last Days' Temple* (Eugene, OR: Harvest House, 1996).

7. For more indications of the signs of the time see Tim LaHaye, "Twelve Reasons Why This Could Be the Terminal Generation," in *When the Trumpet Sounds,* pp. 427-44.

8. Ed Hindson, *Final Signs: Amazing Prophecies of the End Times* (Eugene, OR: Harvest House, 1996), pp. 35-38.

CHAPTER 7

1. For an extensive commentary on the book of Daniel we recommend John F. Walvoord, *Daniel: The Key to Prophetic Revelation* (Chicago: Moody Press, 1971). This work is complemented by Walvoord's commentary on Revelation, *The Revelation of Jesus Christ* (Chicago: Moody Press, 1963).

2. John F. Walvoord, *Prophecy Knowledge Handbook* (Wheaton, IL: Scripture Press Publications, 1990), p. 233.

3. Donald K. Campbell, *Daniel: Decoder of Dreams* (Wheaton, IL: Victor Books, 1977), pp. 86-87.

4. Ibid., p. 108.

5. One of the most readable and extensive discussions on the chronology of the 70 weeks is found in Harold W. Hoehner, *Chronological Aspects of the Life of Christ* (Grand Rapids: Zondervan Publishing House, 1977), pp. 115-39.

6. Ibid., p.139.

7. Campbell, p. 112.

8. Walvoord, *Prophecy Knowledge Handbook*, p. 543.

9. Paul N. Benware, *Understanding End Times Prophecy: A Comprehensive Approach* (Chicago: Moody Press, 1995), pp. 253-54.

10. J. Dwight Pentecost, *Things to Come: A Study in Biblical Eschatology* (Grand Rapids: Zondervan, 1958), pp. 336-37.

11. Walvoord, *Prophecy Knowledge Handbook*, p. 593.

12. Charles H. Dyer, *World News and Bible Prophecy* (Wheaton, IL: Tyndale House Publishers, 1993), p. 141.

CHAPTER 8

1. Charles Clough, *Dawn of the Kingdom* (Lubbock, TX: privately printed, 1974), p. 15.

2. Robert L. Thomas, *Revelation 8–22: An Exegetical Commentary* (Chicago: Moody Press, 1995), pp. 179-80.

3. Ibid., p. 181.

4. Ibid.

5. Sir William Ramsay, *The Letters to the Seven Churches* (New York: A. C. Armstrong & Son, 1904), p. 107.

6. Thomas, p. 182.

7. Ibid., p. 183.

8. Thomas, p. 185.

CHAPTER 9

1. Neil Postman, *Technopoly: The Surrender of Culture to Technology* (New York: Alfred A. Knopf, 1992), p. 15.

2. Ibid.

3. Cornish, p. 2.

4. Cliff Stoll, quoted in "Who's Plugged into the Future?" *Philadelphia Inquirer,* January 21, 1996, p. H 01 (taken from the Internet). For an interesting comparison of views on the personal impact of computer technology on our lives, see

(New York: Anchor Books, 1995) and Nicholas Negroponte, *Being Digital* (New York: Vintage Books, 1996).

5. Ibid.

6. "Visa, MasterCard Agree on Internet Security," USA Today, February 1, 1996 (from the Internet).

7. Marsha Walton, "New Security Device May Broaden Business of the Web," Cable Network News Home Page, January 16, 1996,from the Internet.

8. Comtex Scientific Corporation, "A Cashless Society Could be in Our Future," Knight-Ridder Wire Services, December 15, 1994 , from the Internet.

9. Thomas McCarroll, "No Checks. No Cash. No Fuss?" *Time*, May 9, 1994, vol. 143, from the Internet.

10. Ibid.

11. Quoted by Steven Levy, "E-Money (That's What I Want)." unpublished paper (1996), p.2, from the Internet.

12. McCarroll.

13. David R. Warwick, "The Cash-Free Society," *The Futurist*, November-December, 1992, p. 19.

14. Ibid.

15. Joel Kurtzman, *The Death of Money* (Boston: Little, Brown & Co., 1993), pp. 180-81.

16. Ibid., p. 181.

17. Ibid., p. 183.

18. McCarroll.

19. Anne Wells Branscomb, *Who Owns Information?* (New York: BasicBooks, 1994), p. 16.

20. McCarroll.

21. Amy Barrett, "Patrolling the Black Holes of Cyberspace," from the Internet.

22. Levy, pp. 2-3.

23. Cited by Levy, pp. 4-5.

24. Kurtzman, p. 194.

25. M.J. Zuckerman, "Terrorism on the Net," *USA Today,* June 5, 1996, p. 1A.

CHAPTER 10

1. Clifford Stoll, *Silicon Snake Oil: Second Thoughts on the Information Highway* (New York: Doubleday, 1995), p. 96.

2. Albert Borgmann, "The Meaning of Technology," *The World & I,* March 1996, p. 298.

3. Gates, *The Road Ahead*, p. 250.

4. Ibid., p. 273.

5. Ricardo Saludo with Assif Shameen, "Ruler of Our Lives?" *AsiaWeek,* November 3, 1995, p. 3, from the Internet.

6. Everette E. Dennis, foreword to *Who Owns Information: From Privacy to Public Access,* by Anne Wells Branscomb (New York: Basic Books, 1994), p. vii.

7. Branscomb, p. 8.

8. Steven Levy, "E-Money (That's What I Want), ibid., unpublished paper (1996), p. 2, from the Internet.

9. Quoted by Levy, pp. 11-12.

10. Alvin Toffler, *Powershift: Knowledge, Wealth, and Violence at the Edge of the 21st Century* (New York: Bantam Books, 1990), p. 20.

11. Russell Chandler, *Racing Toward 2001: The Forces Shaping America's Religious Future* (Grand Rapids, MI: Zondervan, 1992), p. 46.

12. Carl F.H. Henry, *Has Democracy Had Its Day?* (Nashville: ERLC Publications, 1996), p. vii.

CHAPTER 11

1. Carl F.H. Henry, *God, Revelation, and Authority,* vol. IV: *God Who Stands and Stays: Part Two* (Waco, TX: Word Books, 1983), p. 297.

CHAPTER 12

1. For a concise presentation of the millennial kingdom, see the authors' *The Truth About the Millennium,* in The Pocket Prophecy Series, Eugene, OR: Harvest House, 1996.

2. David L. Larsen, *Jews, Gentiles, and the Church: A New Perspective on History and Prophecy* (Grand Rapids: Discovery House, 1995), pp. 310-11.

3. John F. Walvoord, *The Millennial Kingdom* (Findley, OH: Dunham Publishing, 1959), p. 318.

4. Ibid., p. 319.

5. Carl F.H. Henry, *Carl Henry at His Best: A Lifetime of Quotable Thoughts* (Portland, OR: Multnomah Press, 1989), p. 28.

6. Ibid., p. 24.

CHAPTER 13

1. Carl F.H. Henry, *Twilight of a Great Civilization* (Westchester, IL: Crossway Books, 1988), p. 143.

RECOMMENDED READING

The resources listed below are among the many works cited in the chapter notes and are recommended for those who want to pursue the issues we discussed. Inclusion in this list does not necessarily imply complete agreement with the contents of the titles, nor are all of the works in the notes cited.

Bacard, André. "A Cash-Free Society: Nirvana or Nightmare?" *The Humanist,* January-February, 1994, pp. 41-42.

Benware, Paul N. *Understanding End Times Prophecy: A Comprehensive Approach.* Chicago: Moody Press, 1995.

Borgmann, Albert. "The Meaning of Technology." *The World & I,* March 1996, pp. 289-99.

Branscomb, Anne W. *Who Owns Information? From Privacy to Public Access.* New York: BasicBooks, 1994.

Campbell, Donald K. *Daniel: Decoder of Dreams.* Wheaton, IL: Victor Books, 1977.

Chaum, David. "Achieving Electronic Privacy," *Scientific American,* August 1992, pp. 96-101.

Cook, Terry L. *The Mark of the New World Order.* Indianapolis, IN: Virtue International Pub., 1996.

Cornish, Edward. "The Cyber Future: 92 Ways Our Lives Will Change by the Year 2025." Bethesda, MD: World Future Society, 1996.

Dyer, Charles H. *World News and Bible Prophecy.* Wheaton, IL: Tyndale House Publishers, 1993.

"Electronic Money: So Much for the Cashless Society." *The Economist,* November 26, 1994, pp. 21-23.

Gates, Bill. *The Road Ahead.* New York: Viking Penguin, 1995.

Henry, Carl. F. H. *Carl Henry at His Best: A Lifetime of Quotable Thoughts*. Portland: Multnomah Press, 1989.

_____. *Has Democracy Had Its Day?* Nashville: ERLC Publications, 1996.

Hindson, Ed. *Final Signs: Amazing Prophecies of the End Times*. Eugene, OR: Harvest House, 1996.

Hoehner, Harold W. *Chronological Aspects of the Life of Christ*. Grand Rapids, MI: Zondervan Publishing House, 1977.

Ice, Thomas and Demy, Timothy. *The Truth About Antichrist and His Kingdom*. Eugene, OR: Harvest House, 1996.

_____. *The Truth About the Millennium*. Eugene, OR: Harvest House, 1996.

_____. *The Truth About the Tribulation*. Eugene, OR: Harvest House, 1996.

_____. *The Truth About the Rapture*. Eugene, OR: Harvest House, 1996.

_____. *The Truth About the Last Days' Temple*. Eugene, OR: Harvest House, 1996.

_____, eds. *When the Trumpet Sounds*. Eugene, OR: Harvest House, 1995.

Kurtzman, Joel. *The Death of Money*. Boston: Little, Brown & Co., 1993.

Lalonde, Peter and Lalonde, Paul. *The Mark of the Beast*. Eugene, OR: Harvest House, 1994.

Levy, Steven. "E-Money (That's What I Want)," unpublished paper, p. 1, acquired on the Internet (steven@echoync.com).

Lynch, Daniel C. and Lundquist, Leslie. *Digital Money: The New Era of Internet Commerce*. New York: John Wiley & Sons, Inc., 1996.

Mitchum, Carl. "Technology and Ethics: From Expertise to Public Participation." *The World & I*, March 1996, pp. 315-29.

Negroponte, Nicholas. *Being Digital*. New York: Vintage Books, 1996.

Postman, Neil. *Technopoly: The Surrender of Culture to Technology*. New York: Random House, 1992.

Ryrie, Charles C. *The Final Countdown*. Wheaton, IL: Victor Books, 1982.

_____. *Revelation*. Chicago: Moody Press, 1968.

Stoll, Clifford. *Silicon Snake Oil: Second Thoughts on the Information Highway.* New York: Doubleday, 1995.

Tapscott, Don. *Digital Economy: Promise and Peril in the Age of Networked Intelligence.* New York: McGraw-Hill, 1996.

Thomas, Robert L. *Revelation: An Exegetical Commentary.* 2 vols. Chicago: Moody Press, 1995.

Walvoord, John F. *Daniel: The Key to Prophetic Revelation.* Chicago: Moody Press, 1971.

_____. *Major Bible Prophecies: 37 Crucial Prophecies That Affect You Today.* Grand Rapids, MI: Zondervan Publishing House, 1991.

_____. *The Prophecy Knowledge Handbook.* Wheaton, IL: SP Publications, 1990.

_____. *The Revelation of Jesus Christ.* Chicago: Moody Press, 1963.

Warwick, David. "The Cash-Free Society." *The Futurist,* November-December 1992, pp. 19-22.

ABOUT THE AUTHORS

Thomas Ice is executive director of the Pre-Trib Research Center in Washington, D.C. He is a frequent radio and conference speaker and the author of numerous books and articles on theology and prophetic issues. Among his works are *Ready to Rebuild,* The Pocket Prophecy Series, and *When the Trumpet Sounds,* all published by Harvest House. He has also contributed articles in *Issues in Dispensationalism,* and the *Dictionary of Premillennial Theology.*

Before assuming his present position, Thomas pastored churches for 13 years in Oklahoma and Texas and served as a chaplain in the Army National Guard. Thomas received his B.A. from Howard Payne University, Th.M. in historical theology from Dallas Theological Seminary, and Ph.D. from Tyndale Theological Seminary. He and his wife, Janice, have been married 24 years and have three sons, Daniel, Timmy, and David.

Timothy Demy is a military chaplain presently assigned in Newport, Rhode Island. He and Thomas are coauthors of The Pocket Prophecy Series and coeditors of *When the Trumpet Sounds,* published by Harvest House. He has also authored and coauthored several other titles and articles, including essays in the *Dictionary of Premillennial Theology,* and the *Dictionary of Evangelical Biography.* Timothy received his B.A. from Texas Christian University and Th.M. and Th.D. in historical theology from Dallas Theological

Seminary. Additionally, he earned an M.A. in European history from the University of Texas at Arlington and an M.A. in Human Development from Salve Regina University. He is currently pursuing a Ph.D. in humanities and technology. He and his wife, Lyn, have been married 18 years.